Rubbing fat into flour for pastry and crumbles

Put flour, salt (if used) and fat, cut into 1 in cubes, into large bowl. Turn fat in flour to coat

Lift up flour and fat, rub between first two fingers, crushing fat into flour. Continue until it is as fine as indicated in the recipe

Separating eggs

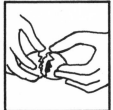

Have ready bowl for yolks, larger one for whites. Tap egg smartly on bowl edge

Tap on 'equator' for equal halves. Pull shell apart gently, holding over bowl

Tip yolk from one half-shell to other, letting white slide out into bowl

When all white is out of shell, tip yolk into smaller bowl

Basting meat

or Stewed fruit

Tip roasting tin so that juices flow to one side

Dip in spoon, fill with liquid and pour over. Repeat as necessary

Tip pan so fruit goes to one side. Dip spoon in among fruit to fill with juice for basting

Boiling

Simmering

Draining

Surface should be covered constantly with bubbles

Few bubbles on surface together. They disappear, more follow after 30 secs

Take pan to sink. Tilt lid to retain contents

Tilt pan, holding lid in place, and let liquid pour out

The First-time Cookbook

" eat, drink & be merry,
fur tomorrow ...."

THE FIRST -TIME COOK BOOK

EVELYN & JUDI ROSE

 Robson Books

FIRST PUBLISHED IN GREAT BRITAIN IN 1982 BY
ROBSON BOOKS LTD., BOLSOVER HOUSE, 5-6
CLIPSTONE STREET, LONDON W1P 7EB. COPY-
RIGHT © 1982 EVELYN AND JUDI ROSE

British Library Cataloguing in Publication Data

Rose, Evelyn
  Quick, easy and delicious recipes for the first
  time cook.
  1. Cookery
  I. Title   II. Rose, Judi
  641.5   TX717

  ISBN 0-86051-184-7

Printed in Hungary

Contents

Introduction

Acknowledgements

We should like to thank the following of Judi's friends who gave special help in testing and commenting on the recipes in this book and the way in which they were set out: Sarah Angel; Mark D. Phillips; Naomi Wolfe and Caroline Whyte. In addition we would like to thank those many College friends of Judi's who tasted her experiments and were free in their (generally) constructive criticisms.

Myer Rose, who though an enthusiastic gourmet is a non-cook, stood in for the older generation of first-time cooks and was particularly helpful in suggesting ways of improving the clarity of the recipes, as was our very supportive editor, Susan Rea.

We should also like to thank Mary Bagnall who was very helpful in the devising of a working system for the book and Sybil Shields who not only typed the final manuscript but also made many useful suggestions to improve it.

Introduction

This book has its genesis in the months that my daughter, Judi,
spent at a university abroad, before coming back to Clare College,
Cambridge. In that time she began to experiment and develop
new recipes of her own and, back in England, many of her
friends were moving into self-catering accommodation at College,
or starting their working life away from home. They asked for her
advice – and indeed mine – on how to cook for themselves in the
easiest (and tastiest) way.

At the other end of the age scale, my husband and I have many
friends who, in middle life, suddenly found the necessity – for
one reason or another – to start cooking for themselves for the
first time.

To meet the needs of all these first-time cooks, we decided to
pool our knowledge and experience and write a book that would
be suitable for the novice cook of any age. Some of the recipes
have been selected from my repertoire, while others are those
Judi has developed herself, using the most basic of cooking
facilities.

We have taken special care to write the recipes in a way which
demands of the reader no basic knowledge of cookery whatsoever,
yet is we hope interesting and exciting enough to stimulate
further interest in culinary skills. So whilst we have given exact
advice on the main basic cooking methods, we have also included
recipes and ideas for cooking for friends in a rather more
elaborate way.

We hope this book will open wide the door for our readers into
the magic world of well-cooked delicious food.

Evelyn Rose 1982

1. Kitchen Orders

Neither of us is particularly tidy by nature, but we have discovered from bitter experience that without some method in the kitchen you get into such a mess that it tends to make you lose your enthusiasm for cooking altogether. In addition, however good the recipe, if it is not followed with care you can't expect to get good results. So we give here the kitchen methodology we have found really works.

1. Some time before you start to cook (ideally the day before), read the recipe carefully so that you can be sure to have the right ingredients and utensils ready – or you can have time to improvise.

2. Just before you start to cook, read the recipe again from beginning to end, and go over each process in turn in your mind.

3. Get out all the ingredients and utensils mentioned in the recipe. Line them up on your working top.

4. Set the oven (if used).

5. Weigh and measure each ingredient with care. To do this with accuracy you will need

   a. Reliable scales

   b. Tablespoons and teaspoons (we use imperial rather than metric spoons). Remember that all our spoons are level unless otherwise indicated

   c. A glass or plastic liquid measure. This is marked at intervals of 1 or 2 fluid ounces or 25 millilitres.

6. Fill a jug and washing-up bowl with hot water and detergent. As you finish with utensils, put them to soak – tools in the jug, basins etc in the bowl. Those that you will need again in the same recipe can be rinsed and left to drain.

7. Start to cook, doing each stage in the order in which it is given in the recipe (we've listed all ingredients in the order in which they are used). Work at a steady pace, but never rush or things are likely to go wrong, especially when it's the first time you've made a particular dish.

8. If there's time before you eat, wash all the cooking utensils and leave them to drain after rinsing under the hot tap – they will then be dry and ready to put away before the main washing-up is done after the meal. If there is no time, leave the utensils soaking in detergent and hot water, and they can then be rinsed out afterwards.

BON APPETIT!

Measurements

Solid measures are given in spoons, pounds and ounces and their metric equivalents. *Never* confuse the two, but use one or the other. All *spoon* measurements are level unless stated otherwise. (For approximate equivalents to one ounce (25 grams) see below.)

Liquid measures are given in spoons, pints and fluid ounces and their metric equivalents. Never confuse the two, but use one or the other.

20 fluid ounces   = 1 pint = 575 millilitres
10 fluid ounces   = ½ pint = 275 millilitres
5 fluid ounces ⎤
                 ⎬ = ¼ pint = 150 millilitres
8 tablespoons   ⎦

Abbreviations
tbsp(s) = tablespoon(s)
tsp(s) = teaspoon(s)

Imperial:
oz   = ounce(s)
lb(s) = pound(s)
in   = inch(es)
fl.oz = fluid ounce(s)

Metric:
g   = gram(s)
kg = kilogram(s)
cm = centimetre(s)
ml = millilitre(s)
l   = litre(s)

Handy measures
We really believe that a pair of accurate scales is essential in the kitchen. However, if scales are not available or the substance to be measured can just as easily be calculated by the spoonful as by the ounce or gram, here are some handy measures that we use in our own kitchen.

All the following are approximately equivalent to 1 oz (25g):
1 level tbsp sugar, rice, warmed syrup
1½ level tbsps caster sugar
2 level tbsps flour, cornflour, icing sugar, fine crumbs
3 level tbsps grated cheese
3 level tbsps raisins or dried fruit
4 level tbsps dried milk
2 level tbsps butter or margarine

Tools for the Job

There is practically no limit to the maximum number of different kitchen tools and utensils that you can buy. There is, however, a *minimum* number you should buy if you wish to cook with any degree of convenience and success (see our list). Of course, kitchen tools don't in themselves make you into a good cook, but a few well chosen pans, bowls, cutlery and 'gadgets' go a long way towards it. Some years ago we ventured into the kitchen of a noted restaurant in a small country town in Central France. The room was dominated by a well-worn scrubbed wooden table and an equally massive – and ancient – gas cooker. The only utensils that were visible were a set of razor-sharp cook's knives, a chopping board and a row of ladles, spoons and whisks hanging above the cooker. Basic indeed, but the food that came from this kitchen was exquisite.

So we are suggesting a minimum list, and then optional extras as you gain interest in certain areas of cookery and perhaps lose interest in others.

As a general rule, don't buy any gadget that has only one function – it isn't worth kitchen space. Whatever utensils you do have, keep within easy reach. Knives are best stored on a magnetic rack fixed to the wall behind the preparation table or counter. Other cooking implements are best kept in some kind of table top holder, which can be as simple as a wide-mouthed jug or as sophisticated as a kitchen 'carousel' which holds thirty to forty implements and spins around as you require it. As a general rule it is better to wait until you can afford the best version of a particular implement rather than buy a cheaper shoddier version. Good kitchen utensils will last a lifetime – we've had many in our kitchen for more than thirty years. This applies in particular to pans – it's not worth buying them unless they have a good solid base that will sit evenly on any kind of cooker – be it gas, electric, ceramic or solid fuel. In addition, make sure that they haven't got any crevices in which dirt can collect.

In our 'minimum' list we mention non-stick pans – *don't* expect these to last a lifetime. However, during their briefer life they will save you untold hours of washing up. But do invest in the 'third generation' of non-stick finishes which has been shown to remain non-stick two to three times longer than previous coatings. The interior is made up of three coats, which are bonded together and to the base of the pan in such a way that if the surface should become scratched, the non-stick finish will not peel off. (The make we are familiar with is called 'Silverstone' and is made by Du Pont. We have found that this finish will stand up to careful use with metal tools such as the batter whisk used for making Cheese and other sauces on pp 50-56).

Essentials
Pans
Non-stick 6 in (15 cm) milk pan with lid
Non-stick 8 in (20 cm) saucepan with lid
Non-stick 8 in (20 cm) frying pan with lid
Non-stick 6 in (15 cm) frying pan (for eggs)
6 pint (3·4 l) soup pan (preferably with lugs rather than handles, so that it can go in the oven as well as on top of the stove)

Pots and bowls
1½-2 pint (850 ml) oven-proof casserole with lid
Large plastic mixing bowl (8-10 in, or 20-25 cm)
Small bowl for beating eggs (6 in or 15 cm)

Cutlery
Bread knife with serrated edge
7-8 in (17·5-20 cm) cook's knife
6 in (15 cm) serrated-edge vegetable knife
Stainless tablespoon, teaspoon, knife, fork
Wooden spoon

Etceteras
Wooden chopping board
Pint (500 ml) measuring jug
Grater
Rubber spatula
Slotted spoon (for draining fried foods)
Can opener
Bottle opener
Garlic press

Soup ladle
Pepper mill
Batter whisk (for making 'all-at-once' sauces)
Scales (most useful are those with dial which can be set back to
zero when more ingredients are added to the scale pan)
Washing-up bowl
Cutlery and plate drainer
Washing-up brush
Pan scrub
Cloths for wiping preparation surfaces
Tea towels
Kitchen rubbish bin

Optional Extras
None of the following are essential basic equipment, but the
'Cooking and Baking' list will enable you to attempt slightly more
ambitious dishes, while the 'Electrical Appliances' are worth
having if someone offers to buy you something for the kitchen.

Cooking and Baking Equipment
Strainer or colander
Roasting tin and rack
Shallow pie plate
Heavy oven trays for making biscuits
11 in × 7 in (27·5 × 17·5 cm) Swiss roll tin
10 in (25 cm) flan dish for kuchens
2 7 in (17·5 cm) sandwich tins
12 × 9 × 2 in (30 × 22·5 × 5 cm) tin
9 in (22·5 cm) loose-bottomed cake tin 3 in (7·5 cm) deep
2 lb (900 g) loaf tin (9 × 5 × 3 in, or 22·5 × 12·5 × 7·5 cm)
Set of 12 patty tins (for little cakes and tarts)
Salad spinner (good for drying smalls, too!)
8 in (20 cm) quiche dish
9 in (22·5 cm) oval gratin dish
Rolling pin
Cooling tray
Scissors
Pastry brush (or 1 in paintbrush)
Stainless steel apple corer
Set of biscuit/pastry cutters
Cake and biscuit storage tins
Storage canisters of 2 lb (900 g), 1 lb (450 g) and 8 oz (225 g)
capacity

Electrical Appliances
BLENDER. Useful if you like a lot of smooth soups and purées.
Don't buy it *as well as* a food processor – the latter can purée
almost as well and can do very much more besides.
FOOD PROCESSOR. Not a luxury, just one of the most successful
kitchen appliances that has been invented in recent years.
Sometimes to be found on special offer, or perhaps for sale by
someone graduating to a larger model.

FRYING PAN. If you have limited cooking facilities, this can be a
life-saver; you can fry, stew, roast and even bake in it if
necessary. Very economical to run.
KETTLE. More economical than boiling water on the stove. Buy
one with a whistle and/or an automatic cut-out.
OVEN WITH AUTOMATIC SETTING. You get the meal ready
before you go out rather than when you return – the oven turns
on to a pre-set temperature at a pre-set time.
SLOW-COOKER. The other way of tackling the problem, if you
can face putting the evening meal on first thing in the morning.
Only uses as much electricity as a light bulb. Food can never
overcook in it.
SANDWICH-MAKER. Fun for snacks. Don't refuse one if it's
offered, but it's not very high on our list.

Pressure Cooker
This can cut cooking times dramatically; it will cook a stew in
twenty to thirty minutes instead of the more usual two to three
hours.

2. Your Daily Food

We firmly believe that the ability to enjoy life to the full depends to a very great extent upon eating well-cooked, easily digested and nutritious meals at reasonably regular hours. If we didn't we wouldn't be writing this book.

It's easy to recognize whether or not your daily food is well-cooked and easily digested, but how do you know if it's nutritious as well? Actually, it's quite easy to discover if it's *not* because there are several very well-documented results of poorly-balanced diets: you may put on excess weight; you may feel listless and lack energy; you may suffer frequently from digestive malaise s including constipation. You may even get depressed.

Yet having to choose any food according to its calorie content and whether or not it contains specific amounts of food nutrients such as vitamins, proteins and minerals is extremely boring and tedious – and is far removed from the joyful attitude to food and cooking that we hope we express in this book.

We have found that a far more pleasant – and equally effective – method of achieving a good daily diet is to think in terms of the servings of specific *foods* you need every day rather than of food *nutrients* and in what proportion. Once you've got a list of these essential foods, it's not difficult to plan meals which use them in dishes that suit both your personal taste and your budget.

Foods which should be eaten every day

Meat, poultry, fish	One or more servings a day.
Eggs	One a day (including those used in cooking and baking) or at least three a week.

Fruit	One serving a day of any fruit, whether fresh, dried, canned, frozen or as juice. *In addition*, one serving of citrus fruit (orange, grapefruit, lemon) or tomato, whether fresh or canned.
Vegetables	One serving a day of a yellow or green vegetable; one serving of a potato or root vegetable; one serving of any raw vegetable, usually in salad.
Milk and Cheese	One pint of milk a day for adults, more for children. This can be served as a drink or included in the cooking. From a nutritional point of view, 1 oz (25 g) of cheese is the equivalent of ½ pint (275 ml) milk.
Fats	Approximately 1 oz (25 g) butter daily, as well as margarine and other fats and oils used in cooking (but we generally eat *too much fat* in this country).
Bread and cereals	Two or more servings of bread, whole grain cereal (such as porridge and breakfast foods) and pasta. (Bread is a good source of protein, the B vitamins and roughage as well as energy-giving carbohydrate.)

NOTE: Vegetarians will need extra servings of eggs, cheese and bread to ensure a sufficient supply of the protein otherwise found in fish, meat and poultry.

Once these basic needs have been satisfied, you can eat whatever else takes your fancy - a gain in weight will soon show when you have been eating too much. Of course, most people do eat rather more than their basic requirements, but this will do no harm provided these extras are made up of protein foods such as meat, fish, poultry and dairy products, as well as foods that are rich in vitamins and minerals, such as fruit, vegetables and whole-grain cereals. But all too often, unless you plan at least one meal ahead, it's easy to satisfy your appetite with sugary or starchy snacks which, because they add nothing to the diet in nutritional terms, are said to contain 'empty' calories.

Of course, a good diet must be a flexible one, allowing for the mood of the moment, and for variations from the normal routine, but if the *ideal* daily diet is always kept in mind, it's easy to compensate for 'bad' days by including extra quantities of foods rich in specific food nutrients on 'good' days.

However, do remember that to be nutritious, meals need not be expensive, for there is as much food value in a 'cheap' but prime food, as in a similar one in the luxury class. For example, braising steak contains the same nutrients as grilling steak, while mackerel has as much food value as salmon. In fact, all foods are best eaten when in season, because they will then be at their most nutritious – and also at the lowest price.

It's as well to remember, however, that the actual food value of *cooked dishes* depends to a great extent on how the *raw ingredients* have been stored and prepared. The vitamin content in particular is very easily destroyed through faulty storage and cooking. To avoid this, all leafy green vegetables should be kept away from the light, which tends to yellow their leaves and thus diminish their content of Vitamin C. Dairy products should also be protected from the light, and as much fresh food as possible – particularly dairy foods, meat, fish and poultry – should be stored in the refrigerator. Besides salad and other fresh vegetables, we also refrigerate roots (such as carrots and parsnips, but not potatoes – they can turn green under refrigeration) as well as ' 'exotica' such as aubergines, peppers, avocados (when fully ripe), soft fruit and melons.

Many of the vitamins present in raw food are destroyed by heat, others are soluble in water. Green vegetables should therefore be cooked as quickly as possible in the minimum amount of water and the cooking liquid then used in soups and sauces. The exception is when vegetables are blanched in large quantities of

water, then reheated later to make cooking for a party easier
– but you can't follow the rules every day! However, it is a
mistake to assume that vegetables are always better eaten raw, for
in practice so much *more* of a cooked vegetable can be eaten at
any one time than of a raw vegetable that, when the total quantity
of, for instance, Vitamin C actually absorbed by the body is
calculated, it may be found to be about the same for cooked as
for raw vegetables (most people would eat more cooked cabbage,
for example, than they would coleslaw).

In fact, when planning your daily food, moderation is always the
best policy and a little of a variety of foods is more sensible than
a slavish adherence to a strict régime.

When fresh foods are scarce, preserved ones, whether they are
canned, frozen or dried, can be very welcome. Of course, their
flavour and food value cannot usually be compared with truly
garden-fresh foods (the exceptions being tomato and citrus
products, cooked meats, fish and poultry). But because of the care
and speed used when they are processed, they are often superior
in every way to many so-called 'fresh' foods bought from a shop.
This is particularly true of frozen fruit and vegetables, which
must be picked at their peak to be processed satisfactorily.

Food Hygiene

The risk of food poisoning from raw animal foods has been
greatly reduced in recent years by stricter regulation of the
manufacturing and marketing process, as well as by increasing use
of freezers and refrigerators. But dangers can still arise from
careless handling. Even if you don't actually get food poisoning,
the toxins in the food may make you feel 'under the weather'.

To guard against this as much as possible, it is necessary to
handle cooked foods, in particular, with special care. Once meat,
poultry and fish have been exposed to any form of heat, they
should be cooked completely, or the raising of the internal
temperature of the food may encourage the growth of bacteria
without being high enough to destroy them. One example is the
partially thawed chicken which *looks* cooked but may harbour
harmful bacteria in the body cavity which has not reached a safe
temperature during the cooking process. All cooked foods which

are not going to be used at once, or are left over from a meal, should be cooled as quickly as possible, covered (to prevent contamination by flies and dehydration) and either refrigerated or stored in a cool larder if there is one. We have given storage times for different foods either in the specific recipe or on pp 23-30 . Incidentally, the reheating of food is not harmful, but should be done quickly yet thoroughly so that the food is not actually recooked yet has reached a high enough internal temperature to kill any micro-organisms which have developed during the storage time.

Budgeting for Food

A food budget is useful, not only in keeping expenditure down to a specific amount, but also in helping to ensure that money is spent in the right proportion and on the most essential foods, no matter how much or how little you have to spend. Without such a plan, it is all too easy for food expenditure to rise without any obvious extra nutrition and enjoyment being gained.

We cannot suggest a specific minimum sum you should spend; much will depend on how often you eat out and how many convenience foods you buy to save time. Start off with an experimental sum that strikes a balance between what you *think* your general budget will stand, and what more experienced friends are spending themselves. After a few weeks you will find that for each kind of food there is a basic minimum you will *have* to spend, plus extras which though not essential are very pleasant to buy. In this way, however tight your final food budget may have to be, your food need not be dull, for when your spending is planned in advance, you may well be able to afford more exciting foods than the disorganized impulse buyer who never has all the right ingredients together at one time, and ends up eating expensive and often boring convenience foods.

There is, however, a place *for* convenience foods in even the tightest budget. When time is short, it can pay to save *time* with prepared foods, rather than to save *money* by making them from scratch, particularly if they can be prepared just as well in a factory. Such foods include frozen and dehydrated vegetables, canned, bottled and dehydrated soups, chicken, vegetable and beef bouillon cubes, ready prepared raw or frozen pastry, bread, cakes, pickled meats and delicatessen. However, the majority of these foods should not be regarded as complete in themselves, but only as ingredients for a dish, or as extras to enliven a meal. For whilst no one ever tires of a home-made dish, a similar one made commercially may soon become extremely boring to eat.

Shopping for Food

Shopping for food is an art which is greatly neglected in this country, whereas in other European countries such as France and Germany, children are taught from a very early age how to select food that is fresh and flavourful. As a result, all adults (including the men) are 'expert' shoppers, and the food on offer is of a consistently high quality. However, new methods of marketing food, particularly through the supermarkets, have led to a great improvement in the standard of every kind of food on sale in this country. But we cannot emphasize too strongly that all the culinary skill in the world is no substitute for quality food. For certain less frequently used foods it's a good idea to patronise a specialist supplier. For example, buy nuts and dried fruit from a health food shop, pasta from an Italian food shop, spices from a large chemist or Indian food shop, soup cereals from a health shop or ethnic grocer. And buy no more of any one food than you can reasonably expect to use whilst it is still in the peak of condition.

Here is a rough guide to how often you need to shop for the different kinds of food you are likely to use.

To buy monthly:
Canned foods of all kinds; frozen foods (if you have a freezer); tea; instant coffee; drinking chocolate; sugar; flour; rice, pulses, soup cereals and pasta; bottled sauces and salad dressings; salt, seasonings and dried herbs; sweet and savoury spices; oils; packeted foods other than biscuits.

To buy weekly:
Butter, eggs, packeted and processed cheese; coffee beans; packeted sweet and savoury biscuits; durable vegetables such as potatoes, carrots, leeks, fresh herbs, onions, green peppers and cucumbers; fruits such as oranges, lemons, grapefruit, apples, bananas, tomatoes.

To buy every three or four days:
Meat and poultry (but only if you have a refrigerator); cored and stoned fruits such as pears and plums, and those best ripened in the kitchen, such as melons and avocados; vegetables such as cauliflowers, peas, cabbage, sprouts and aubergines; hard pressed cheeses (e.g. Cheddar); semi-soft cheese (e.g. Edam); cream cheeses; yoghurt, soured and sweet cream.

To buy daily:
Milk; soft fruits and berries; grapes; fresh corn; mushrooms; cakes; sweet yeast breads; bread and rolls; all fresh delicatessen (including salads, cooked meats and smoked fish); fresh fish, liver; raw minced meat.

Storing Fresh Foods

All fresh foods are perishable and must be stored under the kind of conditions which will ensure that they stay at the peak of freshness for as long as possible, whether in the refrigerator (R), the larder (L) or the larder cupboard (LC).

All perishable foods (with a few exceptions such as under-ripe fruit and potatoes – see details below) can be stored in the refrigerator (average temperature 40-47°F, 4-7°C). Indeed, highly perishable foods (e.g. raw fish and meat) *must* be stored under refrigeration if they are to be safe to eat the next day. At normal refrigerator temperatures the growth of the bacteria and moulds which cause food to go bad are inhibited for a period that may vary from 2-28 days, depending on the nature of the food and its freshness when put into the refrigerator. The coldest part of the fridge (40°F, 4°C) is directly under the freezing unit, or, if there is no freezer compartment, since cold air sinks, on the bottom shelf of the cabinet. It is here that the most perishable food should be stored. The least cold part (47°F, 7°C) is farthest away from the freezing unit and in the door unit, where the less perishable foods (e.g. fruit, vegetables, butter and cheese) should be kept. Whatever the food, however, it must be covered in some way so that it does not shrivel or become discoloured in the cold dry air inside the cabinet, and also to prevent it absorbing flavours and smells from 'stronger' foods. Depending on the kind of food (details below), this covering may be plastic, foil, film or paper.

The traditional larder (average temperature 45-50°F, 7-10°C) was usually sited on a north wall, and was ventilated with cold air from outside. Recent studies have shown that since the widespread installation of central heating, the average temperature in most so-called larders is 62°F, 17°C, and there is no adequate ventilation. Such a larder cupboard is therefore only suitable for short-term storage (up to a week) of the less perishable fruits and vegetables, such as citrus fruits, apples and root vegetables. It can, however, be used for maturing foods like melons, avocados and pears which are actually harvested when under-ripe.

Since it is impossible to be dogmatic about how long any kind of food can be kept in prime condition – because so much will depend on the degree of freshness at the start of the storage time – it is good policy to review the contents of the fridge, the larder, and the larder cupboard every day. Any food that looks or smells even slightly unappetizing, particularly if it is of animal origin, should always be thrown away.

Uncooked Meat (R) or (L)
As soon as possible after purchase meat should either be refrigerated or stored in a really cold larder (not more than 45°F, 7°C).
(R) *position*: Under freezer unit.
Wrapping: Put in special refrigerator meat container or place on plate or tray and loosely cover with film or foil.
Shrink-wrapped meat: Unless it is to be cooked the same day, remove or loosen wrapping and treat as above.
Storage time:

Joints, steaks, chops and other prime cuts	3-6 days
Minced (ground) meat, offal (*very* perishable)	1-2 days
Pickled meats, tongue, sausages (observe 'use-by' date if pre-packed)	2-6 days

NOTE: Do not keep any raw meat in the *larder* longer than 24 hours.

Poultry (R)
Poultry is even more perishable than meat and, for safety's sake, it is advisable to refrigerate it if it is not to be used within 24 hours of purchase.
(R) *position*: In coldest part of cabinet.
Wrapping: Loosely wrap in plastic bag, film or foil (allows air to

circulate and thus maintains quality).

Pre-packed birds: Open bag and remove giblets. Leave bird in bag but do not re-close.

Storage time:

Fresh birds	1-3 days
Frozen birds: Allow to defrost in refrigerator then treat as fresh.	(1-3 days depending on size)

Fish (R)

For optimum flavour, fish should be cooked the day it is purchased or caught. It should be refrigerated as soon as it is brought into the kitchen. Handle with care to avoid bruising flesh. Do not wash until ready to cook.

(R) *position:* In coldest part of cabinet.

Wrapping:

Fresh fish: Wrap loosely in heavy greaseproof paper and put on plate or tray. Smoked fish: Wrap tightly in foil or greaseproof paper.

Storage time:

Fresh fish	Maximum of 1 day
Smoked salmon	3 days
Kippers and smoked white fish	10 days

Dairy Foods

All dairy foods must be kept clean, cool and well covered as they easily absorb 'foreign' odours and their vitamin content is quickly diminished if exposed to light. With the exception of eggs (see below), they are best kept under refrigeration or in a very cold larder.

Eggs (L) (up to 50°F, 10°C) or (R) or (LC) daily supply

Under European Economic Community regulations, all egg cartons are stamped with the packing week (Week 1 = first week in January). To ensure the freshest eggs, always buy the highest week number available.

Position: Whether kept in (L), (R) or (LC), store with the pointed end down. This keeps the egg cell floating at the broad end and helps to conserve freshness.

Wrapping: Keep in original egg carton or in refrigerator door rack. As egg shells are extremely porous, keep well away from 'smelly' foods such as mature cheese and onions.

Storage time:

Egg yolk (in airtight container covered with cold water)	maximum 2 days
Egg white (in airtight container). *Discard if smelly*	10 days
Whole eggs in shell (better to buy weekly)	14 days

Fresh milk   (R) or (L)

It is advisable to buy fresh milk daily and refrigerate immediately or store in cold larder.

(R) *position:* Middle of cabinet or in door rack (do not allow to freeze).

Wrapping: Keep covered, whether in the bottle (with original foil cap) or jug (foil or film) to prevent dust and other foreign bodies contaminating it.

Storage time: 1-2 days

Butter   (R) or (L)

Although some sweet cream butters will keep for up to 6 months if refrigerated straight from the churn, it is advisable to buy any kind of butter on a weekly basis as it may have been in and out of the cold store before it reaches the grocer. Some butters now have a 'sell-by' date on the wrapper. Butter for daily consumption can be kept in the LC.

Position: Middle of cabinet or door storage.

Wrapping: Keep in original wrapper or in covered dish. Foil wrappers keep out the light and therefore conserve freshness and food value more effectively than paper wrappers.

Storage time: (better to buy   1 month
weekly)

Cream   (R)

Cream is particularly susceptible to high temperatures and will deteriorate in a few hours at room temperature. Storage time varies according to the time of year.

(R) *position:* Middle of cabinet (do not allow to freeze as it goes 'grainy' unless whipped.

Wrapping: Keep covered in original carton or decant into airtight plastic container.

Storage time:

Single, double, whipping, clotted, whipped	(summer) 2-3 days (winter) 3-4 days
Soured, yoghurt	7-10 days
Bottled	2-3 days
UHT (keep in larder)	2-3 months
Sterilized (unopened; keep at room temperature)	Indefinitely

Cheese

All cheese must be wrapped in a way that will allow it to 'breathe' without drying out, and protect it from excess heat which causes it to 'sweat'.

Hard cheese   (L) or (R)

There is less likelihood of cheese drying out if it is kept in the larder rather than the refrigerator. However, for storage longer than 24 hours, refrigerate.

(L) *position:* Must be cool, dark and airy, preferably on tiled slab.

(R) *position:* Bottom shelf or door. Remove 2 hours before serving, taking off wrappers of pre-packed cheese.

Wrapping: (L) Use cheese dish with ventilated lid, or place on plate covered with upturned bowl, or wrap loosely in greaseproof paper.

(R) Double wrap, first in greaseproof paper or special cheese paper, then put in plastic bag or container.

Storage time:	
Whole cheese and very hard cheese, e.g. Parmesan (in a very cold larder and in winter, 40°F, 4°C)	Up to 6 months
Portion of cheese (use as quickly as possible)	Up to 10 days
Grated cheese (in airtight container)	Up to 2 weeks

Soft and cream cheeses   (R)

As the moisture content is much higher than in hard cheese, these are much more perishable and should be treated in a similar way to cream. With the exception of cottage cheese, which should be served chilled, remove from the refrigerator one hour before serving.

Position: Bottom of refrigerator (coldest part)

Wrapping: Wrap securely in foil or keep in airtight container.
Storage time (depending on   4-7 days
time of year):

Fruit (R) or (L) or (LC) (up to 3 days only)
Once it is ripe, all fresh fruit (with the exception of the banana)
can be kept in peak condition by storing it in a refrigerator or a
very cold larder (maximum temperature 45°F, 7°C). For short-
term only (up to 3 days) it can be stored in the LC or a fruit
bowl.
(R) *position:* Bottom shelf.
(L) *and* (LC) *position:* In one layer, preferably on ventilated rack.
(LC) *wrapping:* Unnecessary.
(R) *and* (L) *wrapping:* See below.
(LC) *storage time:*   Up to 3 days
(R) and (L) *storage time:*   See below
Note: the following instructions refer to (R) and (L).

Apples and Pears
Both taste better if served chilled, though pears should be kept at
room temperature for $\frac{1}{2}$ hour before serving.
Wrapping: Unnecessary.
Storage time: Up to 10 days (may be kept longer but skin tends to
shrivel).

Stoned Fruit: Peaches, plums etc.
Wrapping: Airtight plastic container in one layer
Storage time: 3-4 days

Lemons
Wrapping: Unnecessary.
Storage time: Whole lemons   3-4 weeks (but skins may
    shrivel)

Cut lemons (tightly foil-   up to 4 days
wrapped)

Oranges, Tangerines, Grapefruit
Refrigerate only if to be kept for more than a week.

Melons and Pineapples
Refrigerate only when fully ripe, as they are ruined if over-
chilled.

Wrapping: Unnecessary for whole fruit. Cover cut surface tightly with film or foil.

Storage time:

Whole fruit	7-10 days
Cut fruit	3-4 days
Sugared fruit	1 day

Grapes

Refrigerate only if to be kept more than 3 days in winter, 2 days in summer.

Wrapping: Place unwashed in plastic bag or airtight container.

Storage time: 4-7 days

Soft fruits

Best eaten on day of purchase but may be stored in airtight container after being rinsed and sugared – for up to 48 hours (though they may lose their 'fresh' texture).

Bananas

Never refrigerate as the texture is ruined and the flesh may go black. Ripen (slowly) in (L) or (quickly) in (LC).

Wrapping: Unnecessary.

Storage time: (according to   1-7 days
ripeness)

Vegetables

All varieties (with the exception of potatoes) keep fresh longer if they can be stored in the refrigerator. Do not wash before storage.

(R) *position:* Bottom shelf.

(L) *position:* On ventilated rack, but no green vegetables except hard cabbage.

(R) *wrapping:* Keep each kind separately in a plastic bag. Store all the bags in special vegetable container. Keep easily-bruised varieties in special container.

(L) *wrapping:* Leave unwrapped unless special instructions are given below.

All green vegetables   (R)

Cabbages, sprouts, cauliflowers, green beans, leeks, peas

Storage time: (according to
freshness):   3-7 days

Root vegetables (except potatoes) (R) or (L)
Carrots, turnips, parsnips, swedes
(R) *storage time:*   Up to 2 weeks

Delicate vegetables (R) or (L)
Courgettes, aubergines, peppers, asparagus, cucumbers,
artichokes.
Wrapping: Wrap tightly in film
or foil.
Storage time: (use as soon as   Up to 5 days
possible):

Mushrooms (R)
Wrapping: Airtight plastic
container
Storage time: (best used on day
of purchase):   1-3 days

Tomatoes
For optimum flavour, these are best ripened at room temperature
(in LC), then used at once, though they may be stored in (R).
Storage time:
(R)   Up to 7 days
(L)   Up to 4 days

Potatoes (L) and (LC)
They must be kept cool and dark, between 50-60°F, 10-16°C.
Too high a temperature causes them to sprout. Too low a
temperature gives them a sweet taste (therefore do not
refrigerate). Unwashed potatoes keep better than washed.
(L) or (LC) *position:* On ventilated rack.
Wrapping: Small quantities in paper bags to protect from light.
Bulk potatoes in sack or large paper bags.
Storage time:
Old potatoes (main crop)   1-2 weeks
Bulk potatoes (up to April)   Up to 2 months
New potatoes   Up to 4 days

Salad Greens and Herbs (R)
These can be kept unwashed for several days either in an airtight
plastic container or lidded aluminium pan. When washed, treat as
below.

Wrapping: After drying thoroughly, store in airtight plastic container.
Storage time:

Salad greens	Up to 48 hours
Herbs (e.g. parsley)	Up to 1 week

In Store

This list has been compiled from experience of college self-catering, but we think it is valid for all those starting out to cook for themselves.

For the Store Cupboard
Sugar (granulated and brown); golden syrup
Flour (plain and self-raising); cornflour
Stock or bouillon cubes (chicken, beef and vegetable)
Mustard (English and French Dijon)
Oil (corn oil can be used for both frying and salad dressings)
Bottled sauces, including soy, tomato ketchup, Worcestershire
Garlic cloves and/or garlic salt
Ground spices (cinnamon, ginger, paprika, nutmeg)
Dried herbs (freeze-dried where possible; chives, mint, Italian herb mixture)
Salt; whole black pepper (in mill); ground white pepper (in canister)
Tomatoes (canned in tomato juice); puree (in can or tube)
Pasta (spaghetti, macaroni, egg noodles, vermicelli)
Rice (Patna, brown, Basmati, Italian risotto)
Porage oats
Raisins
Vinegar (malt and wine)
Peanuts (shelled)
Parmesan cheese (ready grated)
Lemon juice (bottled or canned)

In the Larder or Refrigerator
Eggs
Milk
Cheese (grated)
Butter and margarine
Tomato puree (opened cans)
Lemon juice (opened bottle or can)

French dressing (home-made)
Fresh parsley (in plastic container)

In Vegetable Rack
Potatoes
Onions
Carrots

3. Soup

Please don't skip this chapter because you think it's a waste of time when there are so many cans and packets of soup available. Well, a good pot of really tasty home-made soup can last you for several days, and with an egg or a few sandwiches makes the foundation of an almost instant meal. Soup can always be 'let down' to make enough for the unexpected guest. And if you make soup our way, you'll find it's one of the most nourishing of foods – and very easy to prepare.

Remember that without exception all soups improve in flavour if made several hours – or even a day – before they are required. We're going to suggest first two everlasting soups – the kind that you can top up as the days go by to get a different flavour. One has a base of peas, beans and lentils, the other of shredded vegetables. Then we have a basic cream of vegetable soup that can be varied according to what's in season at any particular time.

NOTE: All the soups can be made vegetarian or not depending on the kind of bouillon cubes you use as a foundation.

Everlasting Winter Soup

Serves 2 people four times, 4 people twice, 8 people once.

This is a ribsticker of a soup, the kind that is marvellous to come home to on a winter's night. It's particularly nourishing because it is made with a basis of pulses which contain second class protein, so you don't need much meat, fish or eggs to turn it into a complete meal. It is very easy to make, but one word of caution: you do need to remember to soak the peas, beans and lentils the night before, or any amount of boiling won't make them tender.

Although most supermarkets sell a wide range of soup cereals, it's a good idea to buy them at the local health food shop which will probably have a quicker turnover. You can also sometimes get a ready-made mixture which saves you buying in a lot of different packs.

Utensils
Large basin; sieve; 6 pint (3·5 l) soup pan or casserole; tablespoon; teaspoon; vegetable knife.

Ingredients
½ lb (225 g) green split peas
¼ lb (125 g) red lentils
2 level tbsps pearl or pot barley
4 level tbsps haricot or butter beans
4 pints (2·3 l) water
4 beef or vegetable bouillon cubes
2 level tsps salt
10 grinds black pepper
2 level tsps dried mixed or fines herbes
2 large carrots
White part of a fat leek
A nice little bunch of parsley

Method
1. *The day before* you intend making the soup, put the green split peas, the red lentils, barley and beans into a large bowl, cover with twice their depth of cold water and leave to soak and swell overnight.
2. Next day, tip the cereals into a fine sieve, then put under the cold tap and rinse them thoroughly until the water that drains from them is quite clear.
3. Put the water and bouillon cubes into the pan, add the rinsed pulses and bring to the boil.
4. Remove as much as possible of the froth that comes to the top, using a tablespoon. Season with salt and pepper, and add herbs (except parsley).
5. Peel the carrots and cut into ⅜ in (1 cm) cubes, cut the white part of the leek from the green, rinse it thoroughly under the tap (as it can hold a lot of grit), then cut across in ¼ in (6 mm) shreds.
6. Add the prepared vegetables and the parsley torn into flowerets, to the soup pan.
7. Bring the water back to the boil, stir well, cover and reduce the heat so that the soup is barely bubbling.
8. Allow to cook in this way for 3 hours, very occasionally

stirring the contents from the bottom of the pan to make sure they do not stick to it as the soup thickens.

9. When the soup is ready it will have become a smooth purée except for the tender little pieces of carrot and leek.

10. Taste and if necessary add more seasonings to your taste. It will taste good today, even better tomorrow.

Optional Extras
Each day you will find the soup has thickened on standing; so add some more water to bring the consistency back to that of thin cream. Then, to vary the flavour – one day add a heaped tablespoon of tomato purée; another day throw in a handful of uncooked vermicelli or Chinese noodles; another day tip in the contents of a packet of chicken noodle soup; another day add curry powder to taste.

Everlasting Summer Soup
Serves 2 four times, 4 twice or 8 once

This delicious soup is naturally much lighter than the winter soup but is equally delicious in its own way. It depends for its flavour and interest on a lovely mélange of vegetables – buy them cheaply at the market on Saturday afternoon. Don't worry if you can't get all the vegetables listed; use a little extra of what you have got. Serve the soup thinly sprinkled with grated cheese and with a hunk of brown bread and butter you will have a complete meal.

Utensils
6 pint (3·5 l) soup pan or casserole; cook's knife; grater; tablespoon; teaspoon.

Ingredients

1 medium onion	1 medium green pepper
½ lb (225 g) hard white cabbage or 4 in (10 cm) section of Chinese leaves	1 tbsp chopped parsley (or 2 tsps dried)
8 outer stalks celery including the leaves	1 tbsp finely cut chives (or 2 tsps dried)
White part of a fat leek	2 tbsps finely cut fresh basil (or 2 tsps dried)
1 large carrot	1 oz (25 g) butter or margarine

1 tbsp oil
3 pints (1·7 l) water
3 vegetable or chicken bouillon cubes

1 rounded tbsp tomato purée
1 tsp salt
20 grinds black pepper
Pinch of sugar

Method

1. Prepare the vegetables first, keeping them in separate piles. Peel and chop the onion; shred the cabbage or Chinese leaves; wash and prepare the celery stalks, and chop into ⅜ in (1 cm) squares; wash thoroughly then shred the leek; peel then coarsely grate the carrot; halve, remove the pith and seeds of the pepper and cut in tiny cubes; chop the herbs.
2. Put the pan on a medium light and heat the fats. When the butter or margarine has stopped foaming, add the onion, stir well, then cover and simmer for 5 minutes until translucent. Uncover and cook without the lid for a further 2 or 3 minutes until the onion turns golden.
3. Add the prepared carrot, celery, leek and green pepper, stir well to absorb the fat.
4. Add the stock (made from the bouillon cubes and water), tomato purée, add seasonings (salt, pepper, sugar) and bring to the boil, then add the shredded cabbage or Chinese leaves.
5. Cover and simmer for 2 hours, uncover, add the herbs and simmer a further 15 minutes. Taste and re-season if necessary.

Optional Extras

Next day, if the soup has thickened through standing, add a little more water, but this is not usually necessary until you get to the last two platefuls. To ring the changes, add two tablespoons of rice then simmer for 20 minutes to cook it. Another day, add a small tin of baked beans, stirring well. Yet another day, throw in a handful of short-cut macaroni or broken-up Italian spaghetti and simmer ten minutes to cook it. Finally, you could divide the soup between the required number of soup plates, and toast some slices of French bread on one side, turn over, butter and spread thickly with grated cheese. Float one or two on each plate of soup, then put under the grill until crisp and bubbly. Serve at once.

Leftovers

If you haven't got a refrigerator, you should boil up leftover soup each day, even if you are not going to use it – then it won't go sour. But it will keep without boiling for 4 days in the refrigerator.

Potage du Jour
Serves 6

We call this 'soup of the day' because in France they just put in any leftover vegetables with a few fresh ones and give the soup a different name daily, depending on which vegetable they have put in in the largest proportion. As long as you have about 3 cups (450 g) of prepared vegetables, it doesn't really matter what they are, but the onion which is sautéed at the beginning gives the soup a gentle sweetness, whilst the potatoes thicken it and give it body. If you have a blender you can make this into a smooth purée but we prefer it with some texture – very convenient because if you cut the vegetables small to begin with it saves the tiresome job of blending or sieving at the end.

Utensils
4-6 pint (2·3-3·5 l) soup pan or casserole; sharp knife; potato peeler; wooden spoon.

Ingredients
2 large potatoes (about 1 lb or 450 g)
1 large carrot
White part of a fat leek
1 medium onion
1 medium green or red pepper (optional but adds extra flavour)
1 oz (25 g) butter or margarine
1 pint (575 ml) water

Pinch powdered nutmeg
1 bayleaf
2 tsps salt
$\frac{1}{4}$ tsp white pepper
1 pint (575 ml) milk
1 tbsp finely chopped parsley or chives (for garnish)

Method:
1. Peel, then slice all the vegetables finely, but grate the carrot (it's nicer that way). You may also prefer to cut the potato into little cubes instead of slicing it. The pepper too needs the seeds removing before shredding.
2. Melt the fat in the pan and immediately it becomes liquid, add all the vegetables. Stir them well together to coat them with the fat, cover and 'sweat' (that is, steam in the fat) for 10 minutes.

3. Uncover, add the water and the nutmeg, bayleaf, salt, sugar and pepper.
4. Cover and simmer until absolutely tender – about 45 minutes.
5. At this stage you can purée it on the blender, or mash down the vegetables with a fork – or leave them as they are.
6. Add the milk and bring to the boil, stirring well.
7. If the soup looks too thick – it should be like pouring cream – add a little more milk or water. If too thin, put a tablespoon of cornflour into a bowl, mix it with 2 tablespoons of milk or water until it's like cream, then add to the soup and bubble for 3 minutes to cook the starch in it.
8. Just before serving add the fresh herbs to garnish.

Variations
Using the same total of vegetables (about 3 cups or 450 g) you can use only 1 potato and add 3 large carrots; or you can omit the carrots and add extra leek; or you can omit the carrots and add 8 stalks of celery (try and get stringless variety). To give extra richness you can tip in a small can (6 oz or 175 g) evaporated milk – it will taste just like cream as the vegetables will mask its sterilized taste.

Leftovers
Milk soups don't last as well as meat or vegetable soups, so use up this soup in 2 or 3 days after making it (one day if kept in a larder cupboard).

Almost Instant Tomato Rice Soup
Serves 2 four times, 4 twice, 8 once

If you can wait twenty minutes, this is a marvellous soup that bears no resemblance to the packeted instant soups whose main ingredient seems to be monosodium glutamate.

Utensils
4 pint (2·3 l) soup pan or casserole; can opener; tablespoon.

Ingredients
3 pints (1·7 l) water
3 or 4 chicken stock cubes
1 medium can (1 lb 3 oz) peeled plum tomatoes in tomato juice
1 tbsp lemon juice
2 tbsps brown sugar

2 rounded tbsps canned or tubed tomato purée

2 level tbsps any kind of rice

Method
1. Put all the ingredients except the rice into the soup pan (sieve the tomatoes or not as you prefer).
2. Bring to the boil, then add the rice.
3. Cover and simmer for 20 minutes.
4. Taste and add additional sugar or lemon juice if necessary.

Leftovers
This soup keeps very well because of the acidity of the tomatoes. It will keep two days in a larder, 4 days in the refrigerator.

4. Eggs

Eggs almost qualify as 'instant food'. They certainly can be called 'fast food' for an omelette shouldn't take longer to cook than 45 seconds from the moment the mixture hits the pan until the finished omelette is ready to eat.

Buying eggs
Under EEC regulations, every box of eggs must have a code number on it to let you know how long ago it was packed. However, as this number is equivalent to the number of weeks that have elapsed since January 1, unless you've got your calculator handy, it's almost impossible to relate this figure to the actual date. My solution is to find the shop – or market stall – that consistently sells fresh eggs and give them your custom. How do you know when an egg is fresh? Break one on to a plate: the yolk should stand plump and separate, surrounded by an even viscous band of white. When it is stale, the yolk flattens and spreads into the surrounding white which looks watery.

All eggs are graded by number, the lower number indicating a larger egg, and a higher price. For most purposes Size 3 – average – is fine, though if you are intending to dine on one egg alone, then it's worth getting a Size 1 or 2. In any case, there are only a few pennies difference in price between the grades, so if you're only buying perhaps 6 or 12 eggs a week, it's not worth worrying about. Eggs that claim to be 'free range' – not produced by battery hens – usually have a few pennies premium on them. If you find them good, then it's worth paying the difference.

Storing eggs
Eggs are perishable, and are therefore better kept under refrigeration if at all possible: but keep a few in a bowl at room

temperature – particularly if you intend to bake with them – for daily use, as they will blend more easily into the other ingredients and whip up to a greater volume. The safest policy is to buy eggs weekly, so that even if you haven't got a refrigerator they will stay edible in a larder cupboard.

Boiled Eggs

Don't laugh – there's a right and a wrong way to do even this simple culinary task. There are two schools of thought on the subject, some belonging to the hot water school and others to the cold. All we know is that eggs plunged into absolutely boiling water will often crack, exuding their contents.

To cook an egg so that the white is set but not toughened and the yolk is viscous rather than runny, we do as follows:

Put the egg(s) (which should be at room temperature, not straight from the fridge) in a small pan and cover with very hot water. Bring to the boil, cover and simmer (gentle bubbles breaking the surface) for exactly 4 minutes. Eat at once. If you cannot, tap the top of the egg so that the shell is slightly crushed – then the egg won't go on cooking.

If you like what the French call 'oeuf mollets' – that is, eggs with a white firm enough to come out of the shell whole and a yolk that is not quite set solid – boil for 6 minutes.

If you want so-called 'hard boiled' eggs, simmer for 10 minutes, then immediately put the pan with the eggs in it under the cold water tap and run the water until the eggs feel cold to the touch. In this way the eggs will not have a nasty band of greeny-grey between the yolk and the white.

Fried Eggs

We don't know how *you* like your fried eggs, but we like them with the white bordered with golden-brown crispiness, and the yolk set with a film over it.

Put a nut of butter in a small frying pan and warm it over a moderate light until it starts to foam. Immediately the foaming has died down, break the egg into it and cook over moderate heat until it looks set and is crispy brown on the edges. Then put a plate or a lid over the pan, and allow the egg to steam for a minute or two, until a fine film covers the yolk. Then lift out carefully with a spatula and eat with gusto! We're glad to report that this is the method favoured by the great French authority on food, Prince Curnonsky, though the only kind of fried egg most Frenchmen seem to know is one cooked in very hot oil. This has its virtues, particularly if you have been making chips. As soon as you've taken the chips out, drop in the egg (carefully or the oil will spit viciously) and let it cook until it looks rather like a ballet dancer's tutu. Lift out with a slotted spoon to allow excess oil to drain back into the pan.

Poached Eggs

We have come to the conclusion that the best way to make poached eggs is in an egg poacher. The best results – firmly set white, creamy yolk – are obtained if the eggs are not put in the poacher until the water in it is boiling. A non-stick poacher is a good investment, as it's then very easy to slip out the eggs and the egg holders are easily washed. Some non-stick egg poachers also have a base which doubles as a non-stick frying pan. If you haven't got a poacher, but *have* got a soup ladle, do as follows: bring a small pan of water to the boil. Butter the inside of the ladle, break in an egg then lower the ladle into the boiling water but do not let the water come over the sides of it. Hold it there until the white looks set, then submerge it in the water until the yolk films over. Lift out, draining off any water in the ladle, and serve. Very effective, if a bit fiddly.

Basic Scrambled Eggs
Serves 2

Most people like their scrambled eggs creamy, with a buttery flavour, and for that you need to cook them at a temperature which will ensure that the eggs absorb the butter rather than fry in it. Allow $1\frac{1}{2}$ – 2 eggs per person.

Utensils
Small pan, 5-6 in diameter, (preferably non-stick); fork; knife; wooden spoon; teaspoon

Ingredients
3-4 eggs
½ tsp salt
5 grinds black pepper

1½ tbsp top of milk
½ oz (15 g) butter

Optional extra:
Nut of butter *or* 1 tbsp double cream

Method
1. Break the eggs into a bowl, add the salt, pepper and top of the milk.
2. Using the fork, blend together until the yolks and whites are indistinguishable (about 30 seconds). There's no need for prolonged beating as you don't want a lot of air bubbles which might spoil the texture of the dish.
3. Put the butter into the pan and melt over moderate heat.
4. The moment the butter is melted but before it stops foaming add the egg mixture and start stirring with the wooden spoon. (At first nothing will happen but don't be tempted to turn up the heat.)
5. Keep on stirring all round the sides and the bottom, lifting the pan momentarily off the heat if the mixture seems to be cooking too quickly.
6. When the mixture looks soft and creamily set, it's ready.
7. Drop in the optional extra butter or double cream. This immediately stops any further cooking and gives the eggs a particularly unctuous texture.
8. Pile on hot buttered toast – extra nice if it's been spread with anchovy paste.
9. Immediately fill the pan with *cold* water (hot will set the egg making the pan difficult to clean), and leave to soak until after the meal.

Variations
(Quantities given are for 2 servings – just double for 4)

CHIVE SCRAMBLE (*Basic* recipe, p 41)

Additional Ingredients
2 tsps (1 tsp dried) finely cut chives

Add the chives to the beaten eggs.

CHEESE SCRAMBLE (*Basic* recipe, p 41)

Additional Ingredients
2 tbsps grated sharp cheese

Add the cheese to the scrambled eggs just before serving.

MUSHROOM SCRAMBLE (*Basic* recipe, p 41)

Additional Ingredients
2 oz (50 g) sliced mushrooms

Thinly slice the mushrooms into the melted butter *before* adding
the egg mixture. Fry briskly for 3 minutes, then add the egg
mixture and proceed as for *Basic Scrambled Eggs*.

COTTAGE CHEESE SCRAMBLE (*Basic* recipe, p 41)

Additional Ingredients
2 oz (50 g – about 4 tbsps)   2 tsps (1 tsp dried) finely cut
cottage or low-fat cream cheese   chives

As soon as the eggs begin to thicken, stir in cottage (or cream)
cheese and the chives. Continue to cook until the mixture is the
consistency of whipped cream. Add no further butter or cream.
This is very good if you're dieting as it's high in protein, low in
carbohydrate and very sustaining.

SMOKED MACKEREL SCRAMBLE (*Basic* recipe, p 41)

Additional Ingredients

2 tsps each onion and pepper flakes

4 oz (125 g – about ½ large fillet) smoked mackerel

Scrape the mackerel off the skin and divide into flakes, using a fork. Add all the additional ingredients to the egg mixture, then proceed as in *Basic Scrambled Eggs*. This is sustaining enough for a main meal.

SAUSAGE OR FRANKFURTER SCRAMBLE (*Basic* recipe, p 41)

Additional Ingredients

1 tbsp oil
1 tbsp water

2 cooked sausages or frankfurters

Omit butter and milk from *Basic Scrambled Eggs* recipe.

Mix the eggs with 1 tbsp water, add sausages or frankfurters sliced ½ in (1 cm) thick with salt and pepper, and cook as before except that oil rather than butter is used. This makes a lighter scrambled egg to go with the sausages.

Basic French Omelette
Serves 2

This is the familiar variety where beaten eggs are cooked until set and golden brown underneath, then folded over and served plain or stuffed with a savoury mixture. This is in contrast to the German *pfannkuchen* and the Spanish *frittata*, where the eggs are always *mixed in* with such ingredients as vegetables or smoked sausage, then finished under the grill. There is yet another style of omelette – the 'omelette soufflé' which has the whites beaten to a stiff froth then folded into the yolk mixture.

Large omelettes never seem to be quite as successful as small omelettes, so we rarely make a French omelette for more than 2 people – one can always make a succession of omelettes if there are more guests as each one takes such a short time to cook. You can make an excellent omelette for 1 person, using one egg (for a snack) or 2 eggs (for a main dish).

Utensils
Bowl; fork; teaspoon; medium sized frying pan, rounded at the point where the base meets the sides (this helps to roll the omelette in the pan when it is ready); small knife (for cutting butter); flexible spatula.

Ingredients

3-4 eggs
½ tsp salt
5 grinds black pepper
2 tsps cold water

½ oz (15 g – a large nut) butter
Tiny nut of extra butter (for glazing when ready)

Method
1. If you are going to fill the omelette, prepare the filling before making the omelette, then keep it warm. Make sure your guest is ready to eat as the omelette must be served hot off the pan or it will go tough.
2. Break the eggs into a bowl and add the salt, pepper and water. Beat with a fork until the yolks and whites are blended (don't use a rotary whisk as it will beat in too much air and spoil the texture of the omelette).
3. Turn the heat on under the empty pan and heat for 2 minutes. Have to hand a fork and a flexible spatula. When you can feel a comfortable heat on your hand held 2 in (5 cm) above the pan, add the large nut of butter.
4. The minute the butter stops frothing and turns a pale fawn in colour, add the egg mixture.
5. Immediately start to tilt the pan with one hand whilst you push the cooked edges towards the centre with the fork held in the other, so that the liquid uncooked eggs can flow towards the sides of the pan.
6. When the top of the omelette is set but still creamy, add the filling (if any) in a thick band down the centre of the omelette. With both filled and plain omelettes, tip the pan slightly to the side so that the omelette will roll up (use the spatula to help it if necessary).
7. Now lift the omelette and slip the tiny nut of butter underneath it.

8. Allow to cook a further 30 seconds or until the underside of the omelette is glazed and golden.
9. Either serve from the pan or roll on to a warm dish and serve from that.

Variation I: Additions to the egg mixture

MIXED HERB OMELETTE (*Basic* recipe, p 44)

Additional Ingredients
1 tbsp any combination of
chopped fresh parsley, chives,
tarragon (or 2 tsps dried fines
herbes)

Add to the *Basic French Omelette* before cooking.

CHEESE OMELETTE (*Basic* recipe, p 44)

Additional Ingredients
2 oz (50 g) grated cheese or
2 tbsps low-fat cream cheese

Spread on the top of the *Basic French Omelette* just before folding it – the heat of the omelette will be sufficient to heat the cheese.

CROUTON OMELETTE (*Basic* recipe, p 44)

Additional Ingredients
1 large slice white or brown   1 tbsp oil or large nut butter
bread cut in ½ in (1 cm) cubes

Method
Melt the butter or oil in the omelette pan and add the cubes of bread. Fry briskly until golden brown on all sides. Add a further small nut of butter to the pan and the minute it turns pale fawn, pour in the egg mixture and make the omelette as described in the *Basic French Omelette*.

POTATO OMELETTE (*Basic* recipe, p 44)

Additional Ingredients

1 small cooked potato or one peeled raw potato, cut in tiny cubes

½ oz (15 g – a large nut) butter
2 tsps chopped parsley (or 1 tsp dried parsley)

Melt one large nut of butter in the omelette pan over moderate heat. The moment that foaming subsides, add the potato. If the potato is raw, cover the pan and allow the potato to both fry and soften in the steam. If the potato is cooked, there is no need to cover the pan. In either case, cook the potato until crisp and brown. Add the parsley to the egg mixture. Add a second nut of butter to the pan and the minute it turns pale fawn add the egg mixture and cook as for *Basic French Omelette*.

CRISPY CHEESE OMELETTE (*Basic* recipe, p 44)

Additional Ingredients

2 generous tbsps grated sharp cheese

1 small nut butter

This is a maverick as it's neither an addition to the raw mixture nor a filling. In addition, it breaks all the culinary rules as grated cheese is actually subjected to high heat. However, it's quite delicious.

Make the omelette as described in the *Basic French Omelette*. When the omelette is creamily set on top and ready to fold, scatter thickly with the grated cheese and press it down with a fork on to the surface of the omelette. Lift up a corner of the omelette and slip the small nut of butter underneath. Flip the omelette over so that the cheesey side is on the bottom of the pan. Continue to cook until the underside looks crisp and crunchy. Serve flat (not rolled).

ONION OMELETTE (Basic recipe, p 44)

Additional Ingredients

1 small onion
1 tbsp oil

Pinch salt, black pepper and nutmeg

Skin, then chop, the onion. Put the oil in the omelette pan and, when you can feel the heat on your hand held 2 in (5 cm) above the surface, add the onion, stir well to coat with the oil, then cover and cook for 5 minutes until tender. Uncover and continue to cook over medium heat until a rich golden brown. Sprinkle with the seasonings and stir well. Put the nut of butter used in the *Basic French Omelette* into the pan and, the minute it turns pale fawn, add the egg mixture and cook as for the *Basic French Omelette*.

NOTE: If you are cooking for one, simply add 2 tsps onion flakes to the egg mixture.

Variation II: Omelettes with Fillings

MUSHROOM OMELETTE (*Basic* recipe, p 44)
Serves 2

Utensils
Small vegetable knife; small saucepan (non-stick if possible); tablespoon; wooden spoon; bowl; fork; teaspoon; frying pan; flexible spatula.

Additional Ingredients

¼ lb (125 g) mushrooms	Pinch garlic salt
½ oz (15 g) butter	Good pinch salt and black
1 level tbsp flour	pepper
5 fl oz (150 ml) milk	2 tsps chives (or 1 tsp dried)

Method
1. Cut ¼ in (6 mm) off the stalk of each mushroom and discard (this is the bit that was in the compost). Do not peel; simply wipe each mushroom with a damp cloth or rinse quickly under the cold tap, then dab dry.
2. Slice each mushroom very thinly.
3. Melt the butter in the small pan, add the sliced mushrooms and fry briskly for 2-3 minutes.
4. Add the flour and stir well to mix it evenly with the buttery mushrooms; then add the milk and seasonings.
5. Bubble for 2 minutes, stirring all the time to cook the starch in the flour. Leave on a low light.
6. Make *Basic French Omelette*. Add mushroom sauce at stage (6), when the underside is cooked.

7. Arrange the sauce down the centre, and tilt the pan to fold the omelette over.
8. Serve straight from the pan, or roll on to a warm serving dish.

CHICKEN LIVER OMELETTE (*Basic* recipe, p 44)
Serves 2
Utensils
Sieve (if possible) or basin and paper towels; cook's knife;
chopping board; frying pan; tablespoon; fork; bowl; teaspoon;
flexible spatula

Additional Ingredients

3-4 chicken livers   1 tbsp butter or oil
1 small onion

Method
1. Put the livers in the sieve and wash thoroughly. (If you have no sieve, put in basin to wash, then spread on paper towels to remove excess moisture.)
2. Divide the livers into quarters.
3. Peel, then slice or chop the onion.
4. Heat the oil or butter in the frying pan until you can feel the heat on your hand held 2 in (5 cm) above the surface of the pan.
5. Add the onion and sliced livers and fry gently until softened and golden, stirring with the fork.
6. Lift out of the pan and put in a covered dish or basin to keep warm.
7. Wash out and dry frying pan.
8. Make *Basic French Omelette*. (If preferred, oil rather than butter can be used for frying.)
9. Add liver and onion filling at stage (6), when the underside is cooked. Spoon it on top, roll and serve.

5. Cheese Sauce Plus

Once you learn how to make a cheese sauce, you will have the foundation for a host of main dishes. In the easy 'all-in-one' method we give here, the fat, flour, liquid and seasonings are put into the pan *at the same time*, and a batter whisk is used to blend them quickly and easily into a rich sauce with *no lumps in it at all*. Use a well-flavoured cheese which will grate: Cheddar, Lancashire or Edam – whichever you can find most cheaply. The combination of this sauce with pasta, fish or eggs gives a delicious low-cost meal. (For advice on storing cheese, see p 26.) It is essential to use a saucepan with a thick base, or the sauce will 'catch'.

Basic All-in-One Cheese Sauce

Utensils
Knife; tablespoon; measuring jug (or milk bottle); small saucepan; batter or balloon whisk; wooden spoon

Ingredients
1 oz (25 g) soft butter or margarine
1 oz (25 g – heaped tbsp) plain flour
½ pint (275 ml) milk
1 level tsp dry mustard powder
½ tsp salt
Sprinkle of white pepper

4 oz (125 g) grated cheese (saving 2 tbsps, if indicated, for topping casseroles)
Optional extras
4 tbsps top of milk or evaporated milk (for extra creaminess)
2 tsps fresh chopped (1 tsp dried) parsley or chives

Method

1. Put all ingredients except cheese and optional extras into the pan.
2. Turn on heat and whisk gently over medium light until the sauce starts to bubble. At this stage you may want to change to a wooden spoon, as this gets into the corners of the pan better than the whisk. Simmer, stirring or whisking, for 3 minutes. (This stops it tasting floury.)
3. Stir in the top of milk and chopped herbs (if used), and the grated cheese.
4. Remove from heat immediately (over-heating makes cheese stringy).

Variations

Use in any of the ways suggested below. If no grill is available, any of the following dishes can be browned in the oven (Gas 6, 400°F, 200°C) for 20 minutes, or simply served unbrowned – they will be edible, though not as attractive in appearance or quite as delicious.

Leftovers

This *Basic Cheese Sauce* will keep (covered) for 3 days in a refrigerator. It will only keep 1 day, depending on temperature, in a larder cupboard.

CHEESE TOASTS (*Basic* recipe, p 50)
Serves 2-5, depending on appetite

Additional Ingredients

4 large (or 5 medium) slices of bread	1 tsp dry mustard
	2 tbsps beer
2 oz (50 g) grated cheese	1 tsp Worcestershire sauce (optional but very tasty)

Omit top of milk from *Basic Cheese Sauce* recipe

Method

1. Make the *Basic Cheese Sauce*, incorporating extra mustard, beer, Worcestershire sauce and extra cheese at end. Leave to cool and thicken while you toast the bread and butter it.
2. Arrange the buttered toast in one layer in the grill pan, on a baking sheet or foil plate.

3. Divide the cheese mixture between the pieces of toast (cover the edges of the toast well or they will char).
4. Grill gently until golden.
5. For a 'buck rarebit', just before serving top with a poached or fried egg per portion.

EGGS IN CHEESE SAUCE (*Basic* recipe, p 50)
Serves 2-4, depending on appetite

Additional Ingredients
4-6 eggs
2 tbsps grated cheese reserved
from *Basic Cheese Sauce* recipe

Method
1. Put the unshelled eggs into a saucepan, cover with cold or warm water and bring to the boil.
2. Cover and simmer for 10 minutes.
3. Pour off the hot water, and put the pan under a running cold tap until the eggs feel cool. Meanwhile make *Basic Cheese Sauce*.
4. Shell eggs and cut in half lengthways. Arrange in one layer in a 1-1½ in (2·5-4 cm) deep buttered casserole or tin-foil dish.
5. Pour the hot sauce over the eggs, covering them completely, then sprinkle with the extra grated cheese.
6. Grill until brown and bubbly, and serve immediately.

CAULIFLOWER CHEESE (*Basic* recipe, p 50)
Serves 4

Additional Ingredients
1 fine white cauliflower
2 tbsps grated cheese reserved
from *Basic Cheese Sauce* recipe

2 tbsps crushed cornflakes
(optional but nice)

Method
1. Cut all the flowerets with their stalks off the cauliflower and discard the rest. Wash well under the tap.
2. Put ¼ pint (150 ml) water and 1 tsp cooking salt into a lidded saucepan and bring to the boil.
3. Add the flowerets, cover, and cook at a brisk bubble for 10-15 minutes. Meanwhile, make *Basic Cheese Sauce*. Cover and keep warm.

4. After the cauliflower has been cooking for 10 minutes, try piercing the stalk of a floweret with a sharp knife to see if it's tender (the knife should go in easily).
5. Drain well through a sieve, and put the cauliflower in one layer in a 2 in (5 cm) deep greased casserole or foil dish.
6. Spoon the hot sauce over, then sprinkle with the extra grated cheese, or with cheese and cornflakes (if used) together.
7. Grill until golden and bubbly, or bake in the oven (Gas 6, 400°F, 200°C) for 20 minutes.

COURGETTES IN CHEESE SAUCE (*Basic* recipe, p 50)
Serves 2-4

Additional Ingredients

$\frac{1}{2}$-1 lb (225-450 g) courgettes

2 tbsps grated cheese reserved from *Basic Cheese Sauce* recipe

Cut the courgettes crosswise into $\frac{1}{2}$ in (1 cm) slices (no need to peel) and simmer in a little salted water for 5 minutes or until bite tender. Proceed exactly as for *Cauliflower Cheese*.

MACARONI CHEESE (*Basic* recipe, p 50)
Serves 2

Additional Ingredients

2 oz (50 g) short-cut macaroni
2 tbsps grated cheese reserved from *Basic Cheese Sauce* recipe

2 tbsps crushed cornflakes (optional but nice)

Method
1. Bring a medium pan half full of water to the boil.
2. Add 2 tsps salt and then the macaroni, and boil at a brisk bubble with the pan lid half off (this stops water frothing over sides of pan) until the macaroni is bite tender – about 8 minutes.
3. Meanwhile, make *Basic Cheese Sauce*.
4. Drain macaroni and stir into the hot sauce, and put into a 2 in (5 cm) deep greased casserole or foil dish.
5. Mix the grated cheese and cornflakes (if used) together, and sprinkle on top of the macaroni.
6. Brown under the grill or bake in a quick oven (Gas 6, 400°F, 200°C) until bubbling, about 20 minutes. Serve immediately.

MACARONI AND TUNA CASSEROLE (*Basic* recipe, p 50)
Serves 3-4

Additional Ingredients
4 oz (125 g) short-cut macaroni
2 eggs
7½ oz (215 g) can of tuna

2 tsps chopped fresh (1 tsp dried) parsley

Method
1. Hard-boil the eggs for 10 minutes (see p 40).
2. Meanwhile make Macaroni Cheese as described in the previous recipe, but using 4 oz (125 g) macaroni. Keep warm.
3. Shell eggs, and chop up roughly; drain tuna and flake with a fork so that there are no lumps left.
4. Add tuna to the macaroni and cheese, together with chopped eggs and parsley, and stir thoroughly.
5. Turn into a 2 in (5 cm) deep greased casserole or foil dish.
6. Brown under the grill until bubbly or bake in the oven (Gas 6, 400°F, 200°C) for 20 minutes. Serve immediately.

CHEESE RICE AND TUNA (*Basic* recipe, p 50)
Serves 3-4

Additional Ingredients
7½ oz (215 g) can of tuna
1 cup (8 fl. oz, 250 ml) *cooked* rice (Use ⅓ cup, 2½ oz, 65 g raw rice; see p 136 for how to cook)

3 eggs, hard-boiled (see p 40) and sliced
½ red or green pepper, seeded and chopped finely (optional)
Pinch ground nutmeg
10 grinds black pepper

Reserve 2 tbsps cheese from *Basic Cheese Sauce* for topping.

Method
1. Hard-boil eggs; shell and slice when cooked and cooled. Cook rice if necessary.
2. Meanwhile make *Basic Cheese Sauce*, but reserving 2 tbsps cheese.
3. Drain and flake the tuna as in previous recipe.
4. Stir cooked rice, sliced eggs, chopped green pepper, tuna, nutmeg and black pepper into the cheese sauce.

5. Put into a 2 in (5 cm) deep greased casserole or foil dish, and sprinkle with reserved grated cheese.
6. Grill gently for 10 minutes till rich golden brown and bubbly, or bake in the oven (Gas 6, 400°F, 200°C) for 20 minutes. Serve immediately.

FISH MORNAY (*Basic* recipe, p 50)
Serves 4

Additional Ingredients

4 6 oz (175 g) fillets of haddock or cod, defrosted or fresh
1 bayleaf
Sprig of parsley
1 level tsp each salt and sugar

2 oz (50 g) grated cheese
Mashed potatoes: medium packet instant, or make your own (see p 116).

Method

1. Put fish side by side in a large frying pan.
2. Add enough water to half-cover the fish, then add bayleaf, parsley, salt and sugar.
3. Cover the pan (if no lid available, use foil or a plate), and simmer gently for 20 minutes. Meanwhile make *Basic Cheese Sauce*. When the fish is cooked it will look opaque and flake easily when pulled with a fork.
4. Drain with a slotted spoon, and arrange in a 1 in (2·5 cm) heatproof or foil dish. Pour over *Basic Cheese Sauce*.
5. Make up the mashed potato, and spoon round the edge of the dish. Scatter the centre with the grated cheese, and grill gently until golden and bubbly, or bake in the oven (Gas 6, 400°F, 200°C) for 20 minutes. Serve immediately.

FISH PIE (*Basic* recipe, p 50)
Serves 2-3

This can be made with any white fish fillets or (much tastier in our opinion) with smoked or golden fillets. Please note, the fish must be cooked before you make the sauce.

Additional Ingredients

12 oz (350 g) fresh or smoked fish fillets
1 hard-boiled egg, sliced (see p 40)

Pinch ground nutmeg
Mashed potatoes: medium packet instant, or make your own (see p 116).

Method

1. If fillets are smoked, put in a pan, cover with cold water and bring to the boil. Discard the water. This gets rid of excess saltiness.
2. Cover de-salted smoked fish, or fresh fish, with the ½ pint (275 ml) of milk you need to make the *Basic Cheese Sauce*, and bring to the point when you can see steam rising.
3. Cover and leave on a very low heat (*don't* let it boil, or the milk will froth over) for 10 minutes.
4. Drain, reserving the milk.
5. Remove any skin from the fish, then flake with a fork.
6. Make *Basic Cheese Sauce*, using the milk the fish has cooked in.
7. Add the sliced hard-boiled egg, the nutmeg and the flaked fish, and turn into a 2 in (5 cm) deep greased casserole or foil dish.
8. Make up the mashed potato, and spoon over the fish to cover it completely.
9. Bake in the oven (Gas 6, 400°F, 200°C) for 25-30 minutes, or until brown and bubbly.

6. Fish

Providing the cooking smell doesn't become too pervasive, fish can make a quick and delicious meal. Many varieties of fish are now sold ready-to-cook, in either a coating of breadcrumbs or batter. These are most useful providing you select plump fillets rather than thin ones which have too low a ratio of fish to coating.

However, if you wish to prepare and cook fish from scratch then you will probably cook it either *meunière* – that is in a simple coating of flour, fried in shallow fat – or you will grill it, probably the simplest method of all. Here is how you set about it.

Buying Fish
It is wise to find one of the ever-decreasing number of 'wet' (this is the trade name for fresh as opposed to frozen) fishmongers and take his advice. However, many supermarkets now sell pre-packed unfrozen raw fish, and this is a development to be welcomed. Use steaks of fish cut ¾-1 in (2-2·5 cm) thick and fillets cut from at least a 1½ lb (675 g) fish. Small whole fish (such as trout) should weigh between 8-10 oz (225-275 g).

Fish you might choose are steaks of sole, hake, haddock, cod, halibut or large plaice; fillets of plaice, sole, haddock, cod, herring, mackerel or baby halibut; whole trout, small herrings or mackerel. Ask the fishmonger to clean whole fish but leave the head on the trout. This is removed just before serving.

Storing Fish
Fish is extremely perishable, and should be kept no longer than overnight – and then only in a refrigerator. The same applies to cooked fish dishes.

Basic Fish Fried in Butter (à la meunière)
Serves 1 or 2

Utensils
Colander or soup bowl; flat plate or greaseproof paper for flour; tablespoon; knife; teaspoon; medium frying pan; fish slice or slotted spoon; fork

Ingredients
1-2 fillets, steaks or whole fish
Salt
5 grinds black pepper
1 oz (25 g – rounded tbsp) plain flour

1 oz (25 g) butter
2 tsps oil
1-2 tbsps lemon juice
2 tsps chopped parsley

Method
1. Wash the fish under cold running water then leave it to drain either in a colander or over the side of a soup bowl. Sprinkle lightly with salt.
2. Put the flour either on a sheet of greaseproof paper or on a plate.
3. Take up each piece of fish in turn then dip it into the flour, patting it on with the hands so that only a thin coating of flour clings to the fish.
4. Heat the frying pan without fat for 3 minutes then add the butter and oil. (The oil stops the butter overbrowning during cooking.) The minute you see the butter start to foam, lay the coated fish in the pan.
5. Cook at a steady (but not a fierce) bubble for 5 minutes, by which time the underside of the fish will be a golden brown.
6. Carefully turn the fish over using the fish slice or slotted spoon and the fork.
7. Cook the second side for a further 4-5 minutes, then lift out and put on warm plates.
8. Into the fat left in the pan put the lemon juice, parsley, a further pinch of salt and 5 grinds of black pepper. Stir well.
9. Pour over the fish.

TROUT WITH ALMONDS (*Basic* recipe, p 58)

Additional Ingredients
1 or 2 tbsps slivered or split almonds

Add to pan juices at stage (7), after fish has been removed from pan. Allow nuts to brown for a few moments, then add lemon juice, parsley, salt and pepper as directed above.

Basic Grilled Fish
Serves 1-2

Unlike meat, fish does not need a fierce heat, as it is unnecessary to 'sear' the outside to contain the juices . . . too high a heat may well make the fish dry. It does, however, need butter to keep it moist and flavoursome. Select fish of the same size and varieties as when frying in butter.

Utensils
Colander or soup bowl; grill pan or baking dish that fits under the grill and is just large enough to hold the fish (too large a dish, and the uncovered butter burns); tablespoon; fish slice or slotted spoon; knife; fork

Ingredients
1-2 fillets, steaks or whole fish	Flour
1 oz (25 g) butter	Lemon cut in wedges (for
Salt, white pepper	garnish)

Method
1. Wash the fish under running water, and leave it to drain sprinkled with salt as in the previous recipe. Make 3 slanting cuts across the top of whole fish.
2. Put the butter in the chosen dish and put dish under a moderately hot grill.
3. The minute the butter melts, but before it changes colour, lay the fish flat in the dish, then immediately turn it over so that it is coated with butter on both sides.
4. Sprinkle each piece of fish with a little salt and white pepper, and a very light dusting of flour.
5. Grill gently but steadily without turning, allowing 10 minutes for a piece $\frac{3}{4}$ in (2 cm) thick and 12 minutes for one that is

1 in (2·5 cm) thick, or a whole fish.

6. About 2 or 3 minutes before the end of the cooking time, sprinkle with a further dusting of flour and baste with any liquid butter in the dish.

7. When the fish is done, fillets will be a rich golden brown; steaks will also be brown but, in addition, the centre bone will wiggle when gently pulled; the flesh of whole fish will be creamy when a little skin is pulled away and the fish flaked with a fork.

8. Serve with the juices from the grill pan and the wedges of lemon.

Variations

CHEESY GRILLED FISH (*Basic* recipe, p 58)
Serves 1-2
Additional Ingredients

1-2 tbsps salad cream or mayonnaise	supermarkets and good delicatessens)
1-2 tbsps dried breadcrumbs (brown, from good	1-2 tbsps grated cheese

Omit lemon wedges from *Basic Grilled Fish* recipe

This is an excellent way of grilling rather thin fillets of plaice (you will probably need 2 fillets per person); it is suitable for steaks or fillets, but not for whole fish. Proceed as *Basic Grilled Fish* to end of stage (5). Then, omit second dusting with flour. Instead, spread each piece of fish with a thin coating of salad cream or mayonnaise, and sprinkle with the crumbs mixed with the cheese. Continue grilling for another 3-4 minutes until the topping is crispy and brown.

SPICY GRILLED HERRING OR MACKEREL
Serves 1-2
Additional Ingredients

Small nut of butter	5-10 drops Worcestershire
1-2 tsps vinegar	sauce
½-1 tsp dry mustard	Pinch of salt

Omit flour from *Basic Grilled Fish* recipe

Method
1. Prepare fish as for *Basic Fried Fish* (p 58), or *Basic Grilled Fish* (p 59), to end of stage (1).
2. Mix butter, salt and pepper with all additional ingredients except small nut of butter.
3. Grease grill pan or dish with additional butter, and put it under the grill for 3 minutes to heat up, then lay the fish in it side by side.
4. Dab the surface of the fish dry with a paper towel, then spread with the flavoured butter.
5. Grill gently; herring take about 10 minutes, mackerel will take 12.
6. Serve immediately. These are fat fish so the spicy topping makes a refreshing contrast in flavour. No other sauce is needed as it keeps the fish juicy and it will be a lovely rich dark brown.

7. Mince

Approximately thirty per cent of all the meat bought from the butcher's is mince. The main reason is undoubtedly the price; but it is also a most versatile form of meat as it can be made into a multitude of dishes with the minimum of work.

Buying mince
In the USA there are many grades of mince, each prepared for a special purpose – some dishes call for fat mince, others for lean. In this country you will usually find two qualities of mince, the cheaper one usually having a high proportion of fat which can give the resulting dish an unpleasant fatty flavour. As a general rule, buy the best mince the butcher has on offer; or buy chuck or shoulder steak and ask him to mince it for you.

Storing mince
Because it has so many cut surfaces, mince is more perishable than regular cuts of meat and if it cannot be refrigerated it should be cooked the day it is bought. Refrigerate for no more than 24 hours. But it can safely be frozen for up to 3 months. If any mince develops a slightly sour smell, throw it away – it's not worth risking food poisoning. Cooked mince will keep for up to 24 hours in a larder cupboard, and 3 days in the refrigerator. But always reheat it thoroughly before eating it.

Basic Savoury Mince

This is a quickly made but very delicious basic mixture which can be served 'as is' or mixed with rice and pasta or combined with pastry of different kinds to make substantial dishes.

Utensils required

Cook's knife; chopping board; 8 in (20 cm) heavy saucepan with lid; tablespoon; large fork; teaspoon

Ingredients

1 medium onion
1 large green pepper, or 2 tbsps dried pepper
2 tsps fresh chopped (or 1 tsp dried) parsley flakes
2 tbsps oil
1 lb (450 g) lean minced meat

2 rounded tbsps tomato ketchup
2 tsps soy sauce
2 tsps Worcestershire sauce
1 level tsp salt
10 grinds black pepper
4 tbsps water

Method

1. Finely chop the onion, the green pepper (halved, seeds and pith removed) and the parsley.
2. Heat the oil in the pan until you can feel the heat with your hand held 2 in (5 cm) above the surface. Add the onion and pepper and cook until soft – about 5 minutes. Add the meat and continue to cook, stirring with a fork to help it to cook evenly.
3. When the meat has lost its redness, add all the remaining ingredients, put on the lid and simmer for 30 minutes until the meat is tender when tasted and the mixture is juicy but not watery. If it is too liquid, simmer for a few minutes without the lid.
4. The mixture is now ready to serve plain or in a pie or casserole.

NOTE: Don't worry if you haven't got all the seasonings – build up a stock gradually. The mince will still be good, even if not quite as tasty, without some of them.

Variations

SPANISH RICE (*Basic* recipe, p 62)
Serves 4

This is a delicious mixture which can be reheated very easily. Use long-grain (also known as Patna) rice, or parboiled long-grain rice. (See pp 135-7 for hints on cooking rice.)

Additional Ingredients

6 oz (175 g) long-grain rice
¾ pint (425 ml) water
1 stock cube – meat or chicken
1 medium can (1 lb 3 oz or
530 g) tomatoes canned in
tomato juice

2 level tsps brown sugar
1 level tsp paprika
Shake of garlic salt *or* 1 clove
garlic, crushed
1 tbsp lemon juice

Method

1. First cook the rice. Bring the water and stock cube to the boil in the pan, add the rice and stir until it starts to simmer. Cover and cook for 20 minutes. Tip into a basin.
2. Meanwhile, make the *Basic Savoury Mince*, adding the tomatoes, sugar, paprika, garlic salt and lemon juice. Cook for 20 minutes, rather than the 30 specified in the basic recipe.
3. Take off the lid, add the cooked rice and stir gently with a fork to blend rice and mince together. Cover and simmer a further 20 minutes until the mixture is thick and juicy.

CHILI CON CARNE (*Basic* recipe, p 62)
Serves 3-4

Additional Ingredients

1 clove garlic, crushed *or*
sprinkle garlic salt
1 level tbsp plain flour
2 bayleaves
1 tsp chili powder
2 tsps paprika

1 tsp curry powder (optional)
1 tbsp brown sugar
1 15 oz (425 g) can tomatoes
1 15 oz (425 g) can kidney
beans, drained

Omit tomato ketchup, soy sauce, Worcestershire sauce and 4 tbsps water from *Basic Savoury Mince*.

Method

1. Make *Basic Savoury Mince*; add additional ingredients (except kidney beans) at end of stage (2).
2. Simmer for 30 minutes.
3. Add well-drained beans to meat mixture and simmer for 5 minutes until heated through. Serve with potatoes or rice.

NOTE: This is a fairly mild version; add more or less chili powder as you prefer. There are also excellent chili sauces to be bought at most supermarkets. This is a great dish to multiply up for a party.

Leftovers
Keep for 1 day in a cool larder, 3 days covered in a refrigerator.

COTTAGE PIE (*Basic* recipe, p 62)
Serves 4 or 5

A satisfying main dish that is economical and easy to make.

Additional utensils
Potato peeler; ovenproof dish about 7 in (18 cm) diameter, or 7 in (18 cm) square and 2 in (5 cm) deep

Additional Ingredients

1 level tbsp flour	2 level tsps salt
Potato topping	$\frac{1}{4}$ tsp white pepper
2 lbs (900 g) potatoes	3 oz (150 g) margarine

Method
1. Set the oven at Gas 4, 350°F, 180°C if you intend finishing dish in oven, see stage (9).
2. Make the *Basic Savoury Mince* but sprinkle the tbsp of flour on to the meat after it has lost its redness, stage (3). Cook for a further 2 minutes before adding the remaining ingredients.
3. Whilst the mince mixture is cooking, prepare the potato topping as follows: peel the potatoes, cut them into quarters and put them in a pan containing sufficient boiling water to cover.
4. Add the salt, bring the water back to the boil, then cover the pan and cook at a steady boil for 15 minutes, or until a piece of potato feels tender when pierced with a thin vegetable knife.
5. Drain off the water from the potatoes (easiest done by holding the pan over the sink and tilting the lid so the water runs out, but *not* the potatoes).
6. Return the pan with the potatoes to the stove and shake over gentle heat until all the moisture has evaporated.
7. Add the margarine in small pieces and start beating with a large fork. Keep on beating (over a low heat) until the potatoes are smooth and fluffy.

8. Spoon cooked *Basic Savoury Mince* into greased ovenproof dish, pile potatoes on top, smooth level, then make a design on top by running the back of the fork lightly through the potatoes. (This not only makes it look attractive, but produces a crisper finish.)
9. Bake for 30 minutes until golden brown; or, if you have no oven, you can grill gently until golden brown (about 10 minutes).

SPRING MINCE RAGOÛT (*Basic* recipe, p 62)
Serves 3-4

This mixture is excellent served with mashed potatoes or boiled new potatoes, or baked potatoes.

Additional Ingredients
1 red pepper
4 oz (125 g) mushrooms

Pinch of garlic salt or clove of garlic crushed
1 small packet frozen peas

Method
1. Halve the pepper, remove the seeds and white pith, then cut into pieces 1 in (2·5 cm) square.
2. Remove the last ¼ in (6 mm) of the mushroom stalk, then slice very thinly.
3. Make the *Basic Savoury Mince*, adding the red pepper and mushrooms at the same time as the onion and green pepper.
4. Add the garlic with the other seasonings.
5. Cover and simmer for 20 minutes, then remove the lid, add the peas, cover and simmer for a further 10 minutes.

MEAT STRUDEL (*Basic* recipe, p 62)
Serves 4-5

If you can find ready-rolled puff pastry, this dish can be made in minutes. Otherwise you will have to roll the pastry out as thinly as possible.

Utensils
Rolling pin and board (if necessary); baking sheet; pastry brush

Additional Ingredients

1 lb (450 g) frozen puff pastry   Sesame seeds
1 egg, beaten

Method

1. Make *Basic Savoury Mince*; allow to cool.
2. Pre-heat oven (Gas 7, 425°F, 215°C).
3. Either unroll the rolled-out puff pastry or roll out the regular pastry into a rectangle about 14 × 12 in (35 × 30 cm) – it should be thin enough to see the board through.
4. Spread the cooled mince filling evenly all over the pastry to within an inch of each side.
5. Turn this inch border over the mince on the long sides, then roll up the pastry, enclosing the meat in a long roll.
6. Take a baking sheet and hold it under the cold tap, then shake off the excess water but do not dry it.
7. Carefully transfer the strudel, join side down, on to the baking sheet. Flatten it slightly with the palm of your hand – it should now resemble a flattened Swiss roll.
8. Beat up the egg with a fork, then spread it all over the top of the strudel, using a pastry or 1 in (2·5 cm) paintbrush (kept for the purpose).
9. Scatter sesame seeds thickly on top.
10. Make about 6 cuts, 2 in (5 cm) apart, through the top crust. Bake for 15 minutes, then reduce the heat to Gas 6 (400°F, 200°C) and continue to cook for a further 10-15 minutes until a rich golden brown. Serve in thick slices.

Basic Meatballs or Beefburgers
Makes 25-30, according to size

If you have access to a freezer, then it's well worth while making up 3 lbs (1·4 kg) of minced meat into meatballs or beefburgers. *You can store them raw for 4 months.* We're not sure that smaller quantities are worth the time or effort involved – you can get 'American style' all-beef burgers at many of the better supermarkets. That is why we are giving the recipe based on 3 lbs of meat. To freeze, lay side by side on a tray and freeze until solid (about 2 hours), then store in a bag and take out as many as are required at any one time. Defrost 2 hours before cooking.

Utensils

Basin; grater (or blender); large fork; teaspoon

Ingredients

4 large slices from a sliced loaf
2 large (size 2) eggs
1 large onion
1 clove garlic, crushed *or* pinch of garlic salt
2 level tsps salt

¼ tsp ground black pepper
½ tsp mixed dry herbs and seasoned salt *or* MSG (monosodium glutamate)
3 lbs (1·4 kg) finely minced beef

Method

1. Soak the bread in cold water to cover for 3 minutes, then squeeze as dry as possible with your hand.
2. Whisk the eggs with a fork until well blended. Grate the peeled onion coarsely.
3. With a fork, mix together the bread, onion, eggs and seasonings, then stir into the mince meat.
4. Work thoroughly together using the fork, but do not pack the meat mixture into a solid mass or it will be hard. Leave for 30 minutes if possible.
5. It can now be formed into patties or balls, and grilled, fried or stewed as required.

NOTE: Form the balls by rolling some of the mixture between your palms. Form patties or beefburgers by flattening the balls until they are ½-¾ in (1·25-2 cm) thick and about 2-3 in (5-7·5 cm) in diameter.

Variations

GRILLED MEATBALLS OR BEEFBURGERS (*Basic* recipe, p 67)

Allow 2 meatballs or beefburgers per person. Heat gas or electric grill until very hot; follow manufacturer's instructions if you are using a charcoal grill, but again it should be very hot. Brush tops of meatballs or beefburgers with oil, barbecue or Chinese plum sauce, and grill for 6 minutes; turn, then brush again, and grill second side a further 4 minutes until a rich brown. Serve with chips, fried potatoes, or in a hamburger bun.

FRIED MEATBALLS OR BEEFBURGERS (*Basic* recipe, p 67)

Allow 2 meatballs or beefburgers per person. Put enough oil in a frying-pan to film it over. Heat for 3 minutes, then add meatballs or beefburgers. Fry them quickly for 3 or 4 minutes each side, or until they are a rich brown, and serve straight away.

TURKISH MEATBALLS (*Basic* recipe, p 67)
Serves 3-4

Utensils
Deepish frying pan with lid; oven casserole (optional); cook's knife; chopping board; tablespoon; teaspoon

Additional Ingredients

1 medium onion
1 tbsp oil
2 tbsps pine kernels (if available) *or* blanched halved almonds (optional)
1 5 oz (150 g) can tomato purée

½ pint (275 ml) water
1 tbsp lemon juice
1 tbsp brown sugar
1 tsp salt
10 grinds black pepper

Method
1. Defrost 8 meatballs; or if you are starting 'from scratch' make a third of the *Basic Meatball* mixture and form into 2 in (5 cm) diameter balls.
2. Peel the onion, cut it in half and then in very thin slices.
3. Put the oil into the frying pan and heat for 3 minutes – or until you can feel the heat on your hand 2 in (5 cm) above the surface of the pan.
4. Add the onion slices and cook gently for about 5 minutes until limp.
5. Add the meatballs to the pan and cook until the outsides are a rich brown.
6. Add the almonds or pine kernels and continue to cook until they are brown – about a further 2 minutes.
7. Add all the remaining ingredients and bring to the boil. The meatballs should be just covered; if necessary, add a little more water.
8. Cover and simmer very gently for 1 hour. If more convenient, the meatballs and sauce can be transferred to an ovenproof casserole and baked for 1 hour (Gas 3, 325°F, 170°C), then

uncovered and left for the sauce to thicken for a further 15 minutes. Serve with boiled potatoes, rice or boiled noodles (see p 136 or 144).

Poor Man's Steaks
Serves 2-3

Best quality mincemeat is mixed with a careful selection of seasonings (you can add herbs if you wish), then grilled or cooked in a very lightly greased heavy frying pan, top of stove. The result is quite delicious – and of course much cheaper than using conventional steaks.

Utensils
Mixing bowl; tablespoon; teaspoon; fork; cooker grill or heavy frying pan

Ingredients
1 lb (450 g) best quality minced beef
2 tsps tomato ketchup
2 tsps soy sauce
3 drops Worcestershire sauce (optional)

5 grinds black pepper
1 tsp salt
1 tsp yeast extract (e.g. Marmite) or vegetable paste (e.g. Morga, from health-food shops)

Method
1. If you like a smooth texture, ask the butcher to mince the meat twice; if you like it open, only once.
2. Turn the meat into a bowl and mix in all the other ingredients, using a large fork so that the mixture doesn't pack together and become too solid when cooked.
3. Form into 2-3 'steaks', each about ¾ in (20 mm) thick.
4. Put under a hot grill on a greased grill pan (or on a very hot greased frying pan) and cook to your taste. Probably 5 minutes on either side will produce 'steaks' that are cooked through and a rich brown.
5. Serve with salad or hot vegetables.

8. Tomato Ragoût Plus

This delicious mixture, which we generally refer to as 'tomato mush', is easily made by simmering canned tomatoes (enlivened with herbs, spices, tomato purée and/or tomato ketchup) until the mixture has become concentrated both in flavour and consistency. It can then be used as a cooking medium (for fish, meat balls, chicken livers or vegetables) or as a sauce (to serve with grilled or fried meats such as beefburgers, chops and frying steak). The basic mixture can be made more or less spicy or herby, sweet or sour, by varying the flavourings through trial and error; but the proportions we give below have proved generally popular with family and friends of all ages. In any case, always check the seasonings just before serving. Incidentally, because tomatoes are acid, they inhibit food spoilage and so the ragoût keeps extremely well (see below).

Basic Tomato Ragoût

Utensils
Saucepan with thick base or deep frying pan; wooden spoon; tablespoon; teaspoon; cook's knife or scissors (if fresh herbs are used)

Ingredients
1 medium can (1 lb 3 oz or 530 g) tomatoes in tomato juice
2 tbsps tomato ketchup
2 tsps tomato purée (optional but good for flavour)
1 tsp each salt and sugar
10 grinds black pepper

1 level tsp dried Italian or Provençal herb mixture
Good shake of garlic salt, or 1 clove garlic, crushed
1 tbsp dried parsley or 2 tbsps fresh parsley, coarsely chopped

Method

1. Put all the ingredients into the pan.
2. Bring to the boil and bubble uncovered for 10 minutes, stirring occasionally until thick but still juicy.
3. Taste and adjust the seasonings, adding more if you think they are required. Remember, however, that the flavouring will be intensified if the mixture is left to stand for several hours, or if it is used as a cooking medium.
4. Serve as a sauce or cooking medium in any of the ways given below.

Variations

BEEFBURGERS AND PIZZAIOLA SAUCE (*Basic* recipe, p 71)
Serves 2-4

For this dish, unless you have made the *Basic Tomato Ragoût* beforehand, you first fry beefburgers in a pan, then lift them out and make the sauce in the same pan. Then the burgers are returned to the pan and left to simmer in the sauce for 10 minutes – this greatly improves the flavour of both the meat and the sauce. If you know a friendly gardener you can use fresh basil to give the dish the authentic Italian flavour; otherwise use the dried herb.

NOTE: Use either bought beefburgers or home-made ones (see p 67).

Utensils
Lidded frying pan; slotted spoon; large fork; tablespoon; teaspoon

Additional Ingredients:

1 tbsp oil	1 tbsp fresh basil leaves *or*
4-8 beefburgers	1 tbsp dried basil

Method

1. Put the oil into the pan and heat over a moderate light until you can feel the heat when you hold your hand 2 ins (5 cms) above the base of the pan.
2. Slip in the beefburgers (use the slotted spoon). They should sizzle pleasantly as they go in. If there is no sound, the oil is

too cool so whip them out smartly and continue heating it a little longer. If the oil spits viciously, it is too hot, so leave the beefburgers in the pan but immediately turn down the heat.

3. Cook over moderate heat for about 4 minutes on either side, when they should be a rich brown. Lift them out using the slotted spoon and fork and leave in the lid of the pan.
4. Add all the ingredients for the *Basic Tomato Ragoût*, together with the basil, stir well to blend them with the juices and fat left by the beefburgers, then simmer uncovered for 10 minutes until the ragoût is thick but still juicy.
5. Now return the beefburgers to the pan, cover it and simmer very gently in the ragoût for 10 minutes. Serve piping hot.

Leftovers
These can be reheated. They will keep covered for 24 hours in a larder, 4 days in a refrigerator.

BRAISED STEAK, ITALIAN FASHION (*Basic* recipe, p 71)
Serves 2-4

This is a particularly good way to cook stewing or braising steak as the acidity of the tomatoes helps to tenderize the meat. Slow cooking is vital for success so use either a slow cooker or a very low oven setting (see below). If you have no oven then the meat *can* be cooked on top of the stove but you must turn the heat right down so that the ragoût barely bubbles, or the meat will be tough.

Utensils
Chopping board; cook's knife; heavy frying pan; tablespoon; teaspoon; slotted spoon; large fork; lidded ovenproof casserole (optional)

Additional Ingredients

2-4 pieces of braising or stewing steak, each weighing 6 oz (175 g) and cut ¾ in (2 cm) thick
1 tsp salt
5 grinds black pepper
1 tsp oregano

1 large onion, *or* 1 tbsp dried onion flakes
1 tbsp oil
¼ pint (150 ml) any red wine (optional)
1 beef stock cube

Method

1. Ask the butcher to cut the meat for you – top rib or shoulder steak are both excellent. Otherwise, portion it yourself using the cook's knife. Put the salt, pepper and oregano on to a large plate, then turn the meat portions in this mixture, pressing them firmly down so that it sticks to the surface.
2. Peel the fresh onion (if used), cut it in half then slice paper thin.
3. Put the oil into the frying pan and when you can feel the heat on your hand 2 in (5 cm) away from the surface of the pan, use the slotted spoon to place the portions of steak into it and cook very briskly until they are a rich brown on both sides.
4. Push to one side of the pan, add the onion and cook more gently until a rich golden brown – about 5 minutes.
5. Now add all the ingredients for the *Basic Tomato Ragoût* together with the red wine (if used), the stock cube and the dried onion (if used). Bubble uncovered for 10 minutes, stirring occasionally.
6. Either cover with a tight-fitting lid and simmer very, very gently on top of stove for 1½ hours or until the meat feels tender, or (*better*) transfer to an ovenproof casserole and cook slowly (Gas 2, 300°F, 150°C) for 2 hours or until the meat is tender; or transfer to a slow cooker and cook as directed.
7. Serve with plain boiled rice or noodles (see p 136 or 144).

NOTE: Oven-cooked meat has a richer taste as it is *surrounded* with the heat which helps to caramelize the ingredients and this deepens the flavour.

SPAGHETTI BOLOGNESE (*Basic* recipe, p 71)
Serves 4-5

This hackneyed dish can take on new vitality when cooked our way – with great attention paid to the balance of flavourings in what is really a very simple dish. The sauce tastes better every time you reheat it, so don't worry about leftovers – they can be mixed with rice for Spanish Rice, or simply served over mashed potatoes. Don't start cooking the spaghetti until about 20 minutes before the sauce is ready.

Utensils
Large heavy-based saucepan; oven casserole (optional); very large

pan for boiling spaghetti; tablespoon; teaspoon; large fork;
colander or sieve (optional)

Additional Ingredients

1 onion *or* 1 tbsp onion flakes   1 chicken stock cube
1 small green pepper *or* 1 tbsp   1 bayleaf
green pepper flakes
1 carrot   1 lb (450 g) long spaghetti
2 tbsps oil   4 heaped tsps salt
1 lb (450 g) fresh minced beef   1 tbsp oil
4 fl. oz (125 ml) red wine   Parmesan cheese (optional)
(optional)

Method

1. Peel, then chop the fresh onion finely. Halve, remove the
   seeds and pith then cut the fresh pepper into pieces the size
   of a stamp. Peel, then grate the carrot (may be omitted, but it
   adds sweetness to the sauce).
2. Heat the oil in the large saucepan until you can feel the heat
   with your hand held 2 in (5 cm) above the surface. Add the
   fresh onion, green pepper and the carrot and cook briskly
   until a rich golden brown.
3. Add the meat and cook, stirring constantly with the large
   fork, until it loses its redness. Crumble in the stock cube, and
   add the bayleaf.
4. Now add the wine, if used, and bubble fiercely for
   2 minutes. (Although the wine is not essential, if you have
   the remains of a bottle it does improve the flavour.)
5. Add all the ingredients for the *Basic Tomato Ragoût* with the
   dried onion and pepper flakes (if you haven't used fresh
   already).
6. Bubble uncovered for 5 minutes to concentrate the flavour.
7. *Either* cover and cook at a slow simmer (bubbles breaking the
   surface only occasionally) on top of stove for 2-2½ hours (the
   longer the better); *or* transfer to an oven casserole, cover and
   cook (Gas 2, 300°F, 150°C) for 3 hours.
8. When cooking time is up, uncover the sauce – it should be
   like pouring cream, that is thick enough to coat the spaghetti.
   If not, uncover and leave to bubble for 15 minutes longer.
9. About 20 minutes before the end of cooking time, start to
   cook the spaghetti (see p 143).
10. When spaghetti is nicely *al dente*, drain, and pour into

serving dish. Cover with meat sauce and serve with a sprinkle
of Parmesan if liked.

CHICKEN LIVER SAUCE (*Basic* recipe, p 71)
Serves 3-4
Chicken livers make a very economical quick and delicious meal.
They can be served over noodles, spaghetti or boiled rice.

Utensils
Cook's knife; chopping board; sieve (or basin and paper towels);
heavy based saucepan; wooden spoon; teaspoon; tablespoon

Additional Ingredients

1 onion *or* 1 tbsp dried onion flakes	1 green pepper or 1 tbsp green pepper flakes
2 tbsps oil	1 chicken stock cube
½ lb (225 g) chicken livers	

Method
1. If fresh onion is used, peel and chop finely and cook in the oil until a rich golden brown.
2. Remove any membrane or green portions from the livers, then wash in a sieve held under the cold water tap, then cut in two. If no sieve is available, wash in basin and drain on kitchen paper.
3. Add to the pan and cook briskly for a further 5 minutes, turning every now and again until the livers are a rich brown. (If preferred, the whole livers can be browned under the grill instead of fried).
4. Halve, seed and remove pith from fresh green pepper, then cut into 1 in (2·5 cm) squares.
5. Add all the ingredients for the *Basic Tomato Ragoût*, together with the fresh green pepper or the dried pepper and onion flakes (if used) and the chicken stock cube. Bring to the boil, then simmer uncovered for 5 minutes.
6. Cover and simmer for 20 minutes, stirring occasionally.
7. Uncover and if the sauce is too watery (it should be as thick as pouring cream) bubble for 5 minutes.
8. Serve as preferred.

Leftovers
Will keep 24 hours in a larder, 3 days under refrigeration, 3
months in the freezer.

FISH PROVENÇALE (*Basic* recipe, p 71)
Serves 3-4

This is a very tasty way to cook almost any white fish – cod, haddock, filleted plaice or lemon sole. It's best served warm rather than straight from the oven. It can be cooked in a lidded frying pan on top of the stove or in a dish covered with a lid or foil in the oven.

Utensils
Colander or sieve (if possible); lidded frying pan or shallow oven dish; tablespoon; teaspoon

Additional Ingredients
3-4 fillets white fish, about 6 oz (175 g) each
1½ tsps salt
1 medium onion *or* 1 tbsp onion flakes
1 green pepper *or* 1 tbsp
pepper flakes
1 tbsp corn oil
1 tbsp lemon juice *or* cider vinegar
1 tsp sugar
1 bayleaf

Omit Italian herbs from *Basic Tomato Ragoût* recipe

Method
1. Ask the fishmonger to skin the fillets, then wash, sprinkle with salt and leave in the sieve or colander whilst you prepare the ragoût. (If no colander is available, drape the fish over the edges of a plate to drain.)
2. If using fresh vegetables, peel, then finely slice the onion; halve, remove seeds and pith, then finely slice the green pepper.
3. Put the oil in the frying pan and heat for 2 minutes, then add the fresh onion and pepper (if used), cover and allow to 'sweat' gently for 10 minutes. If dried onion and pepper are used, simply add to the hot oil.
4. Quickly add all the ingredients for the *Basic Tomato Ragoût*, the lemon juice or cider vinegar, the sugar and bayleaf. Bring to the boil, then simmer uncovered for 10 minutes – it should be as thick as tomato ketchup.
5. *Either* add the fish to the sauce in the pan, then cover and cook at a very gentle simmer (bubbles breaking the surface only occasionally) for 15 minutes.
   Or put in a shallow ovenproof dish (gratin dish) large enough

to hold the fish in one layer. Cover with the sauce, then with a lid or foil. Bake in a quick oven (Gas 6, 400°F, 200°C) for 20 minutes.
6. *In either case*, uncover and allow to cook a further 10 minutes to thicken the sauce.
7. Serve warm – 15-20 minutes after removing from the heat.

Leftovers
Will keep 1 day in larder, 3 days in the refrigerator.

AUBERGINE PROVENÇALE (*Basic* recipe, p 71)
Serves 3-4

For this delicious dish, it is cheaper to use canned aubergines au naturel. If these are not available, then substitute 1½ lbs (700 g) fresh aubergines, sliced ⅜ in (1 cm) thick (including the peel). Put a thin film of oil in a grill pan, lay as many slices as will fit side by side in it, turn over so that both sides are coated with oil. Grill 3 minutes each side until tender when pierced with a sharp knife, and golden brown. Repeat until all the slices have been grilled, then treat as canned.

Utensils
Cook's knife; chopping board; heavy frying pan; tablespoon; teaspoon; ovenproof casserole

Additional Ingredients

1 onion, or 1 tbsp onion flakes	can aubergine au naturel or
1 tbsp oil	1½ lb (700 g) fresh aubergines
1 tsp Italian seasoning	(see above)
1 oz (25 g) butter or margarine	Salt, black pepper
1 medium (1 lb 3 oz or 530 g)	2 tbsps bought dried crumbs or
	crushed cornflakes

Method
1. If fresh onion is used, chop finely and cook in the oil until soft and golden, stirring frequently – about 5 minutes. If using onion flakes, simply add them to the pan with the oil and additional Italian seasoning.
2. Add all the ingredients for the *Basic Tomato Ragoût*, plus the extra herbs.
3. Simmer uncovered until as thick as ketchup.

4. Take a little of the butter or margarine and lightly spread it all over the bottom and sides of the casserole. Arrange the aubergine in layers alternately with the tomato mixture, sprinkling each layer with a little extra salt and pepper.
5. If cornflakes are used, make them into crumbs by putting in a plastic bag and crushing with something heavy – either a rolling pin or an empty milk bottle.
6. Sprinkle the crumbs on top of the casserole and dot with the remaining fat.
7. *Either* grill very slowly for 5 minutes until golden and crunchy;
   or put in a quick moderate oven (Gas 5, 375°F, 180°C) for 25 minutes, or until golden brown.

Optional extra: You can sprinkle each layer with grated cheese, and mix a couple of tablespoons (total of 4 oz, 125 g) with the dried crumbs before scattering them on top of the casserole.

Leftovers
Can be eaten cold as an hors d'oeuvre. They will keep for 2 days in a larder, 4 days in the refrigerator.

COURGETTES AU GRATIN (*Basic* recipe, p 71)
Serves 3-4

This is a very similar dish to the Aubergine Provençale but is milder in flavour. At the height of the summer season, courgettes can be bought at knock-down prices, as they can be grown outdoors in this country, whereas aubergines are either imported or grown here under glass.

Utensils required
Potato peeler; frying pan; tablespoon; teaspoon; cook's knife; shallow casserole (gratin dish)

Additional Ingredients:
1 tbsp fresh (*or* 1 tsp dried) basil
4 oz (125 g) cheese, grated

1 oz (25 g) butter
1 lb (450 g) courgettes

Method
1. If courgettes are fresh with firm, shiny skin, do not peel. If skin looks coarse, peel with potato peeler.

2. Cut in 1 in (2·5 cm) thick slices.
3. Melt the butter in the pan over moderate heat. The minute it stops foaming, add the courgettes and fry gently until tender and brown on both sides – about 10 minutes (test by sticking in a little knife, it should go in easily).
4. Add the ingredients for *Basic Tomato Ragoût* and the basil, then simmer uncovered for 10 minutes until thick and juicy.
5. Spread a tiny extra bit of butter all over the inside of the gratin dish.
6. Add the courgettes and tomato mixture, then scatter with the cheese.
7. Grill until the cheese is golden and the mixture below is bubbly.

Leftovers
Will keep 2 days in a larder, 4 days (covered) in the refrigerator

POTATO AND AUBERGINE SAUTÉ (*Basic* recipe, p 71)
Serves 4-5

In this filling meatless main course, fried aubergines are simmered in the *Basic Tomato Ragoût*, then layered with fried potatoes and cheese and served out of the frying pan, browned or unbrowned, depending on whether or not you have access to a grill. It sounds complicated but in practice it's quite straightforward to make. Allow 1 hour from start to finish.

Utensils
Cook's knife; chopping board; basin with plate or saucer to cover; large frying pan; potato peeler; grater; 8 in (20 cm) pan with lid; teaspoon; tablespoon
Additional Ingredients

2 aubergines (approximately 8 oz, 225 g each)	4 tbsps oil
Salt	2 lbs (900 g) potatoes
2 large onions	6-8 oz (175-275 g) grated cheese
Good pinch nutmeg	

Omit Italian herbs from *Basic Tomato Ragoût* recipe

Method
1. Half an hour before you want to prepare the dish, take the aubergines, cut off the bit of sharp stalk, then cut in 1 in (2·5 cm) cubes (no need to skin).

2. Put the cubes in a basin, cover with water plus 2 teaspoons of salt. Cover with a plate or saucer (to prevent discolouration from the air), then leave for half an hour.
3. Drain off water, squeeze as much moisture as possible from cubes, and dry. This pre-salting of aubergines can be omitted but you will need twice as much oil when you come to fry them.
4. Peel, then finely slice the onions. Put 2 tbsps oil in the frying pan and when you can feel the heat on your hand 2 in (5 cm) above the surface of the pan, add the onions, mix well with the oil, then cover and cook till limp and golden – about 5 minutes.
5. Add the well dried aubergines, turn down the heat, cover and cook a further 10 minutes, then uncover and brown quickly for a further 5 minutes.
6. Add the *Basic Tomato Ragoût* ingredients and the nutmeg, bubble 5 minutes then cover for a further 10 minutes until thick but still juicy.
7. Meanwhile, peel the potatoes and halve if large. Put in a pan, cover with cold water plus 1 teaspoon salt, cover and boil until tender when pierced with a sharp knife (don't overcook or they will fall to pieces). Drain well.
8. Tip the tomato and aubergine mixture into a bowl. Wash out the pan and dry, then heat the remaining 2 tbsps oil as you did the first.
9. Slice the potatoes 1 in (2·5 cm) thick and add to the hot oil in one layer. Fry till golden underneath – about 5 minutes.
10. Sprinkle the potatoes with half the grated cheese, then cover with the tomato and aubergine mixture.
11. Sprinkle with the remaining cheese, then brown slowly under the grill until crunchy. Serve hot.

Leftovers

These can be reheated, covered, over a gentle heat. This dish even tastes good served at room temperature (but not straight from the fridge). Will keep 2 days in larder or 4 days in refrigerator.

NOTE: As aubergines are perishable under normal greengrocery conditions, you can often buy them cheaply on Saturday afternoons. They should be glossy and firm and will keep that way for a week in the refrigerator.

9. Casseroles and Stews

It's rather difficult to define the difference between a casserole and a stew as in both cases the food, be it animal or vegetable, is simmered slowly in some kind of liquid which both flavours – and tenderizes – the dish. Generally you think of a *stew* as a dish with rather a high proportion of liquid to solid content, originally always cooked on top of the stove. However, many stews are now cooked in what are called 'casserole' dishes . . . so where does that leave you? Let us just say that both casseroles and stews are generally economical dishes cooked for a long time in a covered dish either on top of or inside the stove.

In this chapter we give some recipes for dishes made with vegetables, fish and meat.

Basic Vegetable Curry
Serves 4

You can vary the basic mixture given here by using different combinations of vegetables; try different strengths of curry, different chutneys. The permutations are endless.

Utensils
Cook's knife; chopping board; potato peeler; mixing bowl; saucepan with lid; can opener

Ingredients

1 large onion (7-8 oz or 200-225 g)	1 tbsp turmeric
2 oz (50 g) butter *or* 3 tbsps oil	3 tbsps plain flour
White part of 1 fat leek	½ pint (275 ml) water
8 oz (225 g) tomatoes	1 vegetable stock cube
1 small cauliflower	2 tsps salt
2 large potatoes (7-8 oz or 225 g)	10 grinds black pepper
1 hard, tart apple	2 rounded tbsps mango chutney
2 tsps curry powder	1 large can baked beans in tomato sauce

Method

1. Peel, halve, then slice the onion as thinly as possible.
2. Heat the fat in the pan and when you feel the heat with your hand held 2 in (5 cm) above the pan, add the onions, stir well to coat with the fat, then cover the pan and cook for 10 minutes over low light.
3. Meanwhile, cut off the roots and green part from the leek and discard. Cut the white part down the centre and put under the cold tap to rinse off any grit. Cut in 1 in (2·5 cm) thick slices.
4. Quarter the tomatoes.
5. Cut the cauliflower flowerets from the stalk, which should be discarded.
6. Peel, then cut the potato in 1 in (2·5 cm) cubes.
7. Peel the apple, halve, core then cut in very small pieces.
8. Take the lid off the pan and add all the vegetables, turning them in the fat and onions. Cover for 5 minutes.
9. Mix the curry powder, turmeric and flour together and sprinkle on top of the vegetables, stirring well for a few minutes.
10. Finally add the water, stock cube, salt, pepper and chutney.
11. Bring to the boil, turn the heat down until the mixture is just simmering, cover and cook for 30 minutes or until the vegetables all feel tender when pierced with a sharp knife.
12. Add the baked beans in tomato sauce, stir well to heat through, then serve with brown rice (see p 135).

Red Pepper Ragoût

Serves 2

Pick up a cheap red pepper at the height of the summer season, add an onion and some canned tomatoes and you have a delicious meal for two, to serve hot or cold, with plenty of thick granary bread, butter and cheese.

Utensils

Frying pan or saucepan with lid; cook's knife; chopping board; tablespoon; can opener

Ingredients

1 medium (about 5 oz or 150 g) onion
2 tbsps oil (best if half and half corn and olive oil)
1 large red pepper
1 medium can (15 oz or 425 g) Italian tomatoes canned in tomato juice

1 tsp salt
15 grinds black pepper
½ tsp sugar
½ tsp Italian herbs or Herbes de Provence
2 tsps fresh parsley, chopped *or* 1 tsp dried

Method

1. Peel, then chop the onion finely.
2. Heat oil in pan until you can feel the heat on your hand held 2 in (5 cm) above the surface.
3. Add the chopped onion, cover, then cook until soft and golden over moderate heat – about 10 minutes.
4. Halve the pepper, remove seeds and pith, then cut in 1 in (2·5 cm) strips.
5. Add to the onion, stir well and cook uncovered for 5 minutes.
6. Now add the tomatoes with juice and all the seasonings and bubble uncovered until thick but still juicy.
7. The pepper should be soft enough to bite through easily but not soggy. Serve from the pan – or allow to go cold before serving at room temperature.

Leftovers

Will keep 2 days in a larder, 4 days covered in the refrigerator.

Stove Top Fish Casserole

Serves 2

This is a casserole in the sense that it is a complete main dish in itself, but it is cooked on top of the stove. Simply double the ingredients to serve 4.

Utensils required

Cook's knife; lidded saucepan or frying pan; grater; teaspoon; tablespoon; small basin

Ingredients

½ lb (225 g) coley, cod, haddock or hake fillet
½ medium carrot
¼ medium onion
1 oz (25 g) butter
½ bayleaf

Pinch salt and pepper
1 tsp cornflour
4 tbsps top of milk *or* evaporated milk
¼ lb (125 g) frozen peas

Method

1. Have the fish cut into 2 or 4 portions. Wash, sprinkle with a little salt and leave for the moment.
2. Peel the carrot and the onion.
3. Melt the butter in the pan. The minute it stops foaming, grate in the carrot and onion. Stir well and cook for a minute or two.
4. Now, add the fish and immediately turn it over so that it is coated on both sides in the buttery onion and carrot.
5. Cover the bottom of the pan with water, add the bayleaf, salt and pepper. Cover the pan and cook very gently, with the water barely bubbling until the fish looks milky in appearance – about 20 minutes.
6. Put the cornflour in a small basin and gradually stir in the milk, then add to the pan, mixing it with the pan juices. Simmer 3 minutes.
7. Now add the frozen peas, cover and cook very gently for 5 minutes.
8. Serve immediately with new potatoes boiled in their skins.

Goulash
Serves 4 once, 2 twice, or 1 several times

This is a stew flavoured with paprika – the mild Hungarian pepper, not the fiery cayenne.

Utensils
Cook's knife; saucepan or lidded frying pan; oven casserole (optional); teaspoon; tablespoon; slotted spoon; potato peeler; small pan with lid

Ingredients
2 onions
2 tbsps oil
2 tsps paprika
1 tbsp plain flour
2 tsps salt
10 grinds black pepper

3 tbsps tomato purée
1 lb stewing steak (shin is traditional) cut into 1 in (2·5 cm) cubes
½ pint (275 ml) water
1 lb (450 g) potatoes

Method
1. Peel, then finely chop the onions.
2. Heat oil in frying pan until you can feel the heat on your hand held 2 in (5 cm) above surface of pan.
3. Add the onion, cover and cook at a moderate heat for 10-15 minutes until soft and golden.
4. Now add the paprika, flour, 1 tsp salt, pepper and purée, and stir well. Add the meat and the water, cover and simmer very, very gently for 1 hour, tightly covered. (If preferred, transfer to oven casserole and cook at Gas 2, 300°F, 150°C for 1½ hours.)
5. Meanwhile, peel the potatoes and cut in 1 in (2·5 cm) cubes. Put in the small pan, cover with cold water, add 1 tsp salt, bring to the boil, cover and simmer for 5 minutes, then drain.
6. After the meat has been cooking for the required time, uncover, add the potatoes, stir gently, cover and cook for a further 30 minutes.
7. Serve preferably on a bed of noodles (see p 144).

Leftovers
Will keep 1 day in the larder, 4 days in the refrigerator.

Beef in Beer
Serves 2 or 4

A hearty casserole with a marvellous rich gravy. Simply double
the ingredients to serve 4.

Utensils required
Cook's knife; chopping board; small plastic or paper bag; pan
with lid; oven casserole (optional); tablespoon; teaspoon; slotted
spoon; plate

Ingredients
1 large onion
1 level tbsp flour
1 level tsp salt
5 grinds black pepper
¾ lb (350 g) stewing beef cut
into 1 in (2·5 cm) cubes
1½ tbsps oil
1 tsp brown sugar

½ can light beer
¼ pint (150 ml) water
Pinch garlic salt
1 tsp soy sauce
1 tsp Worcestershire sauce
1 bayleaf
4 oz (125 g) pack mixed frozen
vegetables

Method
1. Peel, halve then thinly slice the onion.
2. In a plastic or paper bag put the flour, salt and pepper. Add
   the meat cubes a few at a time and toss until coated with the
   seasoned flour.
3. Heat the oil until you can feel the heat on your hand held 2 in
   (5 cm) above the surface of the pan, then add the onions,
   cover and cook gently for 10 minutes or until the onion is soft
   and golden. Lift out on to a plate.
4. In the same fat put the floured meat and cook until brown on
   all sides, adding the brown sugar to hasten the process.
5. Return the onions to the pan together with the beer, water,
   garlic salt, sauces and bayleaf. Bring to the boil.
6. *Top of stove:* simmer for 2 hours or until meat is meltingly
   tender, adding the mixed vegetables 15 minutes before meat is
   done.
   In oven: Cook for 2½ hours (Gas 2, 300°F, 150°C), adding
   vegetables for last 15 minutes.
7. Serve with new potatoes cooked in their skins.

Leftovers
Keep for 1 day in the larder, 4 days (covered) in the refrigerator.

Spring Stew with Dumplings
Serves 2

A rich stew with feather-light parsleyed dumplings. To serve 4, simply double the ingredients (but use only 1 egg for the dumplings).

Utensils
Cook's knife; chopping board; small paper or plastic bag; pan with lid; oven casserole (optional); potato peeler; tablespoon; teaspoon; slotted spoon; fork; basin or mixing bowl; small basin or cup

Ingredients
1 tbsp flour
½ tsp salt
8 grinds black pepper
1 tsp powdered mustard
½ tsp ground ginger
¾ lb (350 g) stewing beef, cut into 1 in (2·5 cm) cubes
1 tbsp oil
1 large carrot
1 small onion

½ pint (275 ml) hot water
1 beef stock cube
4 oz (125 g) pack frozen peas

Dumplings
2 oz (50 g) self-raising flour
1 tbsp margarine (½ oz or 15 g)
1 tsp chopped fresh (or ½ tsp dried) parsley
1 egg

Method
1. Put the flour, salt, pepper, mustard and ginger into the bag and shake the meat in it until it is coated with the seasoned flour.
2. Heat fat in the pan until you can feel the heat on your hand held 2 in (5 cm) above the surface. Add the meat, if necessary in two lots (too much crowding of meat in pan will stop it browning nicely). Cook until the meat is a rich brown on all sides.
3. Whilst this is happening, peel the onion and carrot. Chop the onion finely and cut the carrot first into lengthwise ½ in (1·25 cm) strips and then into ½ in (1·25 cm) cubes.
4. Add the onion and carrot to the meat and continue to cook, stirring well until the onion has become golden brown.
5. Add hot water and cube, stir and bring to boil, then turn heat down until liquid is barely bubbling. Put on lid, or transfer to casserole for oven cooking.

6. Simmer for 1½ hours on top of stove, or cook in oven (Gas 2, 300°F, 150°C).
7. Meanwhile, make the dumplings. Put flour and fat (cut in little cubes) into the bowl and stir in the parsley.
8. Rub the fat and flour between the fingers and thumb of both hands until you can't see any lumps of fat bigger than a small pea on the top when you shake the bowl.
9. Put the egg into a small bowl or cup and beat with the fork to blend the yolk and white. (If making double quantity, add 2 tbsps water to egg.)
10. Add egg all at once to the fat/flour mixture and mix to a sticky dough with the fork.
11. When the stew cooking time is up, uncover the stew and drop tablespoonfuls of the dumpling mixture on to the top (they will swell almost double while cooking).
12. Cover and cook for a further 30 minutes.
13. Ten minutes before cooking time is up, drop in the frozen peas.

NOTE: the gravy will be very flavourful but not very thick. If you prefer a thicker gravy, mix 1 tbsp cornflour with 2 tbsps cold water, and stir into the stew. Bubble for 3 minutes top of stove, 10 minutes in the oven.

Leftovers
Will keep one day in larder, 4 days (covered) in the refrigerator.

10. Stir-Frying

The art of stir-frying was one of the first culinary methods devised by civilized man. The cook in question was from China – or to be more precise, from Canton, the home for centuries of the finest, most elegant Chinese cuisine.

With this method of cooking, now much practised in the West, the raw ingredients, be they vegetables, fish or meat, are cut into tiny, even-sized pieces so that they become bite-tender in a matter of minutes when cooked over a brisk fire in a very little hot fat. Not only is time and fuel conserved by this method, but also the flavour and the vitamins in the food, plus a quality lacking in modern processed foods – the crunch.

To stir-fry in the authentic Chinese manner, a special pan – the wok – is used. This is a deep basin of heavy steel or cast iron – there are even non-stick and electric ones on sale – whose high sides retain the heat, and thus help to cook the food with great speed. However, you can still stir-fry using a large frying pan with a heavy machine-ground base.

In most stir-fry recipes the principal food – fish, meat or poultry – is set off by two complementary ingredients, for example pineapple and green pepper. Each is cut to the same shape and size, precisely fried and then glazed with a beautiful sauce. You can make these sauces from scratch – as in some of the recipes below. But you can also buy some excellent factory-made ones, which though they may seem expensive in isolation, are not so when their price is compared with the outlay on the many different ingredients needed for just one sauce.

Soy sauce, one of the constituent ingredients of many Chinese-style dishes, comes in many different makes and qualities. In the best, the dark colour is produced naturally by maturing, in some it is induced artificially. You can only judge which you like best by trying them out individually

Basic Technique of Stir-frying
Serves 3-4

1. Cut in dice or paper-thin slices approximately 12 oz (350 g) of lean meat, fish, seafood or poultry, then toss in a little oil and cornflour.

2. Cut approximately 12 oz (350 g) of the chosen vegetables in the same way.

3. Heat the wok or frying pan empty over high heat for 2-3 minutes, then add 4 tbsps of oil. When very hot, add the vegetables and fry, tossing continuously until tender – about a minute. Drain from the oil while still crisp.

4. Reheat the oil and stir-fry the meat for approximately 2-3 minutes. Add a bottled sauce or the sauce ingredients listed in the recipe and heat thoroughly, making sure the meat is coated with the sauce.

5. Return the vegetables to the pan, taste and add extra salt and pepper if necessary, and then gently turn all the ingredients so that the vegetables are also coated with sauce. Serve at once.

Stir-fried Vegetables
Serves 4

Utensils
Wok or frying pan; cook's knife; chopping board; slotted spoon; tablespoon; fork; medium bowl

Ingredients

1 medium onion	1 tbsp oil
1 medium green pepper	2 tbsps cashew nuts (optional)
1 small cauliflower	3 tsps sesame seeds (optional)
1 tbsp soy sauce	1 carton bean sprouts

Method

1. Peel then quarter the onion, separate layers then cut in 1 in (2·5 cm) pieces.
2. Halve the pepper, remove the seeds and pith, then slice in very thin slivers which should then be cut in half.
3. Break the cauliflower into very small flowerets no bigger than a hazelnut.
4. Put the vegetables in a bowl and toss in the soy sauce. Leave for up to half an hour to marinate.
5. Heat the oil in the wok or frying pan, add the nuts and sesame seeds (if used) and fry for one minute, then add all the remaining ingredients and cook over moderate heat for about 5 minutes, stirring with the slotted spoon from time to time, till lightly cooked but still crisp.
6. Add more soy sauce if desired at the table.

Leftovers
Re-fry or serve cold as a salad. Eat within one day if kept in the larder, 2 days if in the refrigerator.

NOTE: It is possible to buy ready-to-cook frozen stir-fry vegetables.

Chinese Stir-fried Cabbage
Serves 4

Utensils
Small bowl; tablespoon; teaspoon; cook's knife; chopping board; slotted spoon

Ingredients

1 tbsp cornflour	1½-2 lb hard white or Chinese
6 tbsps meat stock (made with	cabbage
¼ cube)	4 tbsps oil
2 tsps salt	

Method

1. Put the cornflour in the small bowl and add the stock and the salt.
2. Shred the cabbage very thinly and stir in the very hot oil for 2 minutes (see *Basic Technique of Stir-frying*).
3. Add the sauce, stir well.

4. Cover with a lid or plate and cook for 5 minutes until bite tender.

Sweet and Sour Stir-fried Vegetables
Serves 4

This recipe is a good one for vegetarians.

Utensils
Wok or frying pan; cook's knife; chopping board; slotted spoon; tablespoon; teaspoon

Ingredients

2 medium onions	½ lb (225 g) bean sprouts
1 large green pepper	1 jar (approx 5 oz or 50 g)
1 red pepper	Sweet and Sour Sauce
4 oz (125 g) mushrooms	4 tbsps currants
Small can pineapple chunks	Very small packet peanuts
4 tbsps oil	

Method
1. Peel the onion, quarter then separate layers and cut in 1 in (2·5 cm) squares.
2. Halve the peppers, remove seeds and white pith, then shred finely.
3. Thinly slice the mushrooms.
4. Drain the pineapple (save juice for drinking or for a fruit salad).
5. Heat the oil till very hot as outlined in *Basic Technique of Stir-frying*, then add onion and stir-fry for 2-3 minutes until golden.
6. Add mushrooms and pepper and stir-fry a further 2-3 minutes.
7. Add the bean sprouts and stir-fry 1 minute.
8. Add sweet and sour sauce and pineapple and bubble 1-2 minutes, stirring well to coat all the ingredients with the sauce.
9. Add the currants and peanuts.
10. Serve on a bed of Chinese noodles (see p 144).

NOTE: If you want to make your own sweet/sour sauce, mix together 1 small tin crushed pineapple (or titbits cut very small, or baby jar of sieved peaches or plums) ½ cup cider vinegar and ¼ cup soy sauce with salt and pepper to taste. Simmer uncovered over a low light for 15 minutes.

Leftovers
Will keep for 2 days in larder, a week in the refrigerator.

Salami and Eggs Chinese Style
Serves 4

Utensils
Wok or frying pan; slotted spoon; tablespoon; teaspoon

Ingredients
3 tbsps oil
12 oz (350 g) packet frozen stir-fry vegetables
4 oz salami (preferably the frying kind), sliced
4 tomatoes, sliced
6 eggs
Pinch salt and white pepper

Method
1. Heat the oil until very hot in the wok or frying pan.
2. Add the vegetables and fry briskly for 3 minutes, stirring frequently.
3. Lay the sliced salami and tomatoes on top, then break the eggs on top of them.
4. Sprinkle with salt and pepper.
5. Put under a hot grill until the eggs are set. If you have no grill, cover the pan for 2-3 minutes until eggs are set.

Sweet and Sour Chicken with Hazelnuts, Hong Kong Style
Serves 4

Buy two cooked breasts of chicken and use them for a quick meal.

Utensils required
Cook's knife; chopping board; wok or frying pan; slotted spoon; tablespoon; teaspoon

Ingredients

2 tbsps hazelnuts
1 medium onion
1 large green pepper
8 oz can (225 g) pineapple
titbits
3 tbsps oil

8-10 oz (225-275 g) cooked
chicken cut in bite-sized pieces
2 tbsps raisins
2 tbsps soy sauce
1 jar (5 oz or 150 g) Sweet and
Sour Sauce, Hong Kong style

Method

1. Coarsely chop the hazelnuts.
2. Peel the onion, halve and then slice thinly.
3. Halve the green pepper, remove seeds and white pith and slice thinly.
4. Drain the pineapple titbits (reserve the juice for something else).
5. Heat the oil until very hot, add the nuts and cook until golden – about 1 minute.
6. Lift out with a slotted spoon and drain on kitchen paper.
7. Reheat the oil and cook the onion until softened and pale yellow (3-4 minutes), then add the pineapple, the pieces of chicken, the raisins, soy and Sweet and Sour sauces, and the nuts. Stir carefully to coat all the ingredients with sauce.
8. Serve with boiled or fried rice (see p 137) or Chinese noodles.

Stir-fried Chicken Breasts
Serves 2

Utensils

Plate for flour; wok or frying pan; slotted spoon; cook's knife; chopping board; tablespoon; teaspoon

Ingredients

1 chicken breast, divided into 2
2 tbsps flour mixed with $\frac{1}{2}$
teasp salt, 5 grinds black
pepper, pinch paprika
3 tbsps oil
3 heads of broccoli cut in 1 in
(2·5 cm) pieces

3 courgettes cut in 1 in
(2·5 cm) chunks
1 tbsp tomato purée
2 tbsps water
1 tbsp light soy sauce

Method

1. Remove any bones from the chicken breasts.
2. Put the seasoned flour on the plate and turn the chicken gently in it so that it is covered with a thin coating.
3. Heat the oil in wok or frying pan till very hot, as outlined in *Basic Technique of Stir-frying*.
4. Add chicken and cook briskly for 5 minutes until a good brown, then turn down the heat and cook for a further 5 minutes until richly brown, and the juices from the chicken run clear when it is pierced with a sharp knife. Remove.
5. Put the vegetables into the pan, fry briskly for 1 minute, then add the purée, water and soy sauce, and continue to cook for a further 5 minutes.
6. Return the chicken to the pan, stir well, then heat until steaming. Serve at once.

Chow Mein
Serves 3-4

This makes an ideal bed on which to serve stir-fried chicken.

Utensils

Frying pan or wok; cook's knife; chopping board; slotted spoon; tablespoon; teaspoon

Ingredients

1 medium onion	½ tsp salt
1 large green pepper	10 grinds black pepper
½ white cabbage	1 clove garlic, crushed
4 oz (125 g) Chinese noodles	1 tbsp soy sauce
(medium egg noodles)	1 tbsp bottled black bean sauce
3 tbsps oil	(optional)

Method

1. Peel the onion, then chop finely.
2. Halve the green pepper, remove seeds and pith, then cut in strips 2 × ¼ in (5 cm × 6 mm)
3. Shred the cabbage, discarding any hard white core.
4. Cook the noodles according to packet directions (some makes only need to be left covered with boiling water to cook them).
5. In the frying pan or wok, heat the oil as in *Basic Technique of Stir-frying*.

6. When very hot, add the shredded cabbage, and stir-fry for 2-3 minutes.
7. Add the onions, green pepper strips, salt, pepper and garlic and cook, stirring for a further 2-3 minutes.
8. Add the cooked noodles and the soy sauce and heat through for 1 minute.
9. Stir in the bean sauce (if used – it gives a marvellous flavour) and heat through. Serve immediately.

11. Chicken

Chicken portions are easily available, fresh or frozen. You can also buy them ready-roasted, which is most convenient when time is of the essence. However, if you have got the time, it is a simple matter (and cheaper) to cook your own. Then there are occasions when you want to cook a whole chicken or a 'steam roaster' (that's a laying bird that's not too ancient) with the minimum of fuss. So in this chapter we give some ideas for cooking joints both top of stove and in the oven, and two methods of cooking a whole bird; and finally, a suggestion for using up the giblets.

One word of warning – if you use a whole frozen bird, make sure it is at room temperature (including the body cavity) before cooking. Half-frozen birds can cause food poisoning.

Leftovers
Cooked chicken will keep for 1-2 days in the larder (depending on the time of the year) and three days, covered, in the refrigerator.

Basic Crumbed and Fried Chicken Breasts
Serves 1-2

Cooked this way, chicken tastes as good as veal. To save egging and crumbing the chicken, buy coating crumbs that already contain vegetable fat.

Utensils
Chopping board; greaseproof paper; rolling pin; plastic bag; frying pan; tablespoon; slotted spoon; fork

Ingredients

1-2 chicken breast fillets
1-2 tbsps lemon juice
Salt and pepper

Coating breadcrumbs
(approximately 1 heaped tbsp
per portion)
2 tbsps oil

Method

1. Lay the fillets on a board and cover with greaseproof paper, then bang with the rolling pin to flatten them as much as possible.
2. Sprinkle on both sides with the lemon juice, and a pinch each of salt and pepper. If possible leave for 15-30 minutes.
3. Put the coating crumbs in the plastic bag, put the poultry pieces in one at a time and shake until well coated with the crumbs.
4. Put the oil in the frying pan and heat until you can feel the heat on your hand held 2 in (5 cm) above it. Put in the coated pieces and cook steadily, turning once until both sides are a rich brown – about 8 minutes altogether.
5. Eat hot from the pan with boiled potatoes and whatever vegetables you fancy, or cold with salad.

NOTE: Turkey breasts can also be cooked very successfully in this way.

Crumbed and Fried Chicken Portions

This is the way to cook pieces on the bone. Do not beat the portions first, simply season them, crumb them and cook as directed for the breasts, but allowing 6 minutes on each side for breast portions, 8 minutes for legs and thighs.

Oven Fried Chicken
Serves 4
This is an excellent way to cook a larger number of portions, and also ensures that the pieces are cooked evenly.

Utensils

Plastic bag, or dish; tablespoon; teaspoon; baking tray

Ingredients

4 chicken portions
4 oz (125 g, about 4 heaped tbsps) coating crumbs with vegetable fat
1 tsp paprika (optional)

1 tsp dried herbs (Herbes de Provence, Italian herbs or mixed herbs)
½ tsp salt
10 grinds black pepper
Sprinkle of garlic salt (optional)

Method

1. Set the oven at Gas 7, 425°F, 215°C. Defrost the portions if frozen, rinse under the tap then dab almost dry (they should still be damp so the crumbs will cling).
2. Put the coating crumbs in the plastic bag or dish and mix with the seasonings.
3. Put each portion in turn into the bag and shake to coat with the crumbs, or turn in the dish.
4. Lay on a greased baking tray, leaving 2 in (5 cm) between the portions.
5. Bake for 40 minutes until a rich brown. Eat hot or cold.

Baked Chicken Parcels

This is a useful way if you want to get the chicken into the oven as quickly as possible and don't want to coat it with crumbs.

Utensils

A square of foil large enough to enclose each portion; cook's knife; chopping board; grater

Ingredients

For each chicken portion:
Salt, pepper, lemon juice
2 tsps grated onion
Few strips of green pepper
1-2 mushrooms, sliced

1 tsp tomato purée diluted with 1 tbsp water, or 1 large tomato, sliced
Sprinkle of herbs (chopped parsley or dried Italian seasoning)

Method

1. Set the oven at Gas 6, 400°F, 200°C and preheat while you prepare vegetables.
2. Lay each piece of chicken on a piece of foil and sprinkle lightly with salt, pepper and lemon juice.

3. Top with the onion, pepper, mushrooms and tomato, and finally sprinkle with the herbs.
4. Fold into a loose but airtight parcel.
5. Bake for 40 minutes.
6. Serve hot with all the lovely juices from each parcel poured on top of the chicken. (To add to the flavour, if you have the time, you could fry the dried portions in a little oil until a rich brown on either side, before adding the other ingredients.)

Roasted Chicken in Foil
Serves 4-6, according to size

This is a very simple way of cooking a bird without any attention. It gives particularly succulent results if you want to eat the bird cold.

Utensils
Piece of foil large enough to cover the bird when *loosely* wrapped round it; tablespoon; teaspoon; pastry brush

Ingredients
1 bird weighing 3-4 lbs
(1·4-1·8 kg)
1 tbsp lemon juice

1 tsp salt
15 grinds black pepper
Oil

Method
1. Pre-heat the oven at Gas 8, 450°F, 230°C. Wash the bird thoroughly, and pour boiling water into the body cavity, to make sure it's absolutely clean. If there are any bloody bits left clinging to the inside, scrape them out with the spoon and discard.
2. Dry the bird thoroughly and sit it in the middle of the foil, breast side up.
3. Sprinkle with the lemon juice, salt and pepper, then coat thinly with the oil (if you have no pastry brush, use your fingers).
4. Wrap into a loose but airtight parcel – a tight one would insulate the bird from the heat of the oven.
5. Bake for 45 minutes, then open the parcel, turn back the foil and let the bird roast uncovered for a further 15-20 minutes or until a rich brown.
6. Serve hot or cold.

Basic Braised Fowl
Serves 4-6, according to size

This is a marvellous way to cook an older bird which can be bought more cheaply than a roaster, though it's not worth doing unless the bird weighs at least 4 lbs (1·8 kg) net. The bird is then cooked on a bed of lightly fried vegetables with a little liquid to produce the steam that an older bird needs to tenderize it. However, it is necessary to have an ovenproof casserole large enough to take the bird. If you haven't, try the *Braised Joints* recipe which follows next.

Utensils
Potato peeler; cook's knife; chopping board; saucer or small bowl; teaspoon; tablespoon; liquid measure or cup; frying pan; oven casserole with lid; slotted spoon; fork; sieve or blender (optional)

Ingredients

1 level tsp salt
Good sprinkle garlic salt
10 grinds black pepper
2 level tsps flour
2 level tsps paprika
1 'steam roaster', minimum weight 4 lbs (1·8 kg)
1 tbsp oil
1 large onion
1 carrot

2 soft tomatoes *or* 1 tbsp tomato purée
1 bayleaf
4 fl. oz (125 ml) chicken soup (see note on p 103) *or* chicken stock (made from a cube)
½ green pepper (optional)
3 stalks celery (optional)
2 oz (50 g) mushrooms (optional)

Method
1. Preheat oven at Gas 4, 350°C, 180°C.
2. Prepare vegetables: peel and slice onion and carrot; if used, slice tomatoes, seed green pepper and cut into strips and slice thinly celery and mushrooms.
3. Mix together in a saucer or small bowl the salt, pepper, flour and paprika. Rub well into the skin of the bird.
4. Heat the oil in the frying pan until you can feel the heat on your hand held 2 in (5 cm) above the surface, then fry the onion until it is soft and golden.
5. Now add the carrot, tomatoes and bayleaf (and optional vegetables if used) and stir over a more gentle heat until they

have absorbed the fat. Add tomato purée, if used.

6. Put at the bottom of the casserole and lay the bird (on its side) on top.
7. Pour the soup or stock down the side of the casserole (if preferred, you could use an equivalent amount of dry red or white wine).
8. Cover the casserole, put it in the oven and leave for 30 minutes, then have a look.
9. If the liquid is bubbling gently, turn the oven down to Gas 2, 300°F, 150°C; otherwise, wait a little longer before reducing the temperature.
10. Cook for a further 2½ hours, basting twice.
11. To serve, lift the bird from the vegetable and juices, skim off as much fat as possible with a tablespoon and either serve the juices 'as is' or push through a sieve or, best of all if you have one, give a whirl on a blender until smooth.

BRAISED JOINTS OF FOWL (*Basic* recipe, p 102)
Serves 6 once, 3 twice
Do it this way if your casserole isn't high enough to take the whole bird. Either buy portions or ask the butcher to joint a bird into 6 sections.

Additional Ingredients
6 good tbsps coating crumbs

Omit flour from *Basic Braised Fowl* recipe

Method
1. Mix the salt, pepper, paprika and garlic salt with the crumbs, then coat the joints with the flavoured crumbs.
2. Lay on top of the fried vegetables and cook as directed.
3. The portions will probably need half an hour less in the oven than the whole bird.

Chicken Giblets
Chicken livers are delicious if grilled or fried quickly, then used as the filling for a French omelette (see p 49).

If you have a freezer, stockpile the other giblets and when you have perhaps three sets use them to make chicken soup. Put all the giblets into a pan with 2 pints (1·2 l) water, 1 whole peeled onion, 2 peeled and sliced carrots and a sprig of parsley, together with 2 chicken stock cubes. Simmer covered an hour or so, then leave overnight for the flavours to develop. Strain and discard solids; cook a handful of egg noodles in the soup for 10 minutes or so before serving. Delicious – and so cheap!

12. Meals in Minutes

For those occasions when you want almost instant food, but want it hot, here are a few suggestions. I have also included some 'dips' or 'spreads' that you can make in reasonable quantity and refrigerate ready for instant use.

Cream Cheese Fritters
Serves 2

These are savoury fritters, ideal for a light lunch. The recipe originated in the early days of the establishment of the state of Israel, when there was very little meat – they used to be known as 'cheese steaks'.

Utensils
Cup or small bowl; fork or batter whisk; medium-sized bowl; tablespoon; teaspoon; frying pan; slotted spoon

Ingredients
1 large egg (size 2 or 3)   ½ tsp each sugar and salt
¼ lb (125 g) curd, cottage or   2 tbsps butter
cream cheese   1 tbsp oil
1 heaped tbsp self-raising flour

Method
1. Break the egg into a bowl or cup and whisk till frothy with the fork or batter whisk.
2. Put the cheese into the medium bowl and gradually add first the beaten egg and then the flour, sugar and salt.
3. Put the butter and oil into the pan over moderate heat. The minute the butter starts to foam, drop tablespoons of the

mixture into the pan, flattening slightly with the back of the spoon.
4. Fry at a gentle bubble until risen and golden brown on one side, then turn and cook until the second side is brown.
5. Serve hot off the pan. Nice with stewed apple, or a couple of tablespoons of caster sugar mixed with a good pinch of cinnamon.

French Toast
Serves 2

This is a very old recipe, eaten everywhere in Europe, but it's really delicious – and very cheap.

Utensils
Fork; small bowl; tablespoon; frying pan; spatula

Ingredients
1 large egg (size 2 or 3)   3 slices white or brown bread
2 tbsps top of the milk   1 oz (25 g) butter
Pinch each sugar and salt   1 tbsp oil

Method
1. With the fork, beat together the egg, milk, sugar and salt.
2. Cut each of the pieces of bread into 4 fingers, then dip in the egg mixture until well moistened.
3. Put the butter and oil in the frying pan and the minute the butter starts to foam, lay as many fingers of soaked bread in the pan as will go side by side. Cook at a gentle bubble until both sides are a rich golden brown, turning once. Serve hot off the pan with cinnamon sugar (see *Cream Cheese Fritters*, stage (5), above).

Hot Cheese Crisps
For any number

These can be made in an electric sandwich grill, but you can make them equally well in a heavy frying pan.

Utensils
Knife for spreading; frying pan; spatula

Ingredients per person

2 large slices of bread
1 slice Gouda or Cheddar
cheese (large enough to cover
bread)

Dijon or Bordeaux mustard *or*
any kind of pickle or chutney
Butter

Method

1. Using *unbuttered* bread, make a sandwich with the cheese, spreading one slice with the mustard, pickle or chutney. Press the slices firmly together.
2. Heat the pan for 3 minutes without fat, whilst you butter one outside of each sandwich with soft butter. After 3 minutes, lay the sandwich buttered side down in the pan, and butter the top of it. Cook gently until the underside is crisp and golden brown, turn and fry the other side.
3. Lift out of the pan, cut in quarters and serve, with some nice fresh tomatoes and a handful of crisps.

Herb and Spice Cheese Spread

A good dip to have on hand if you're watching the calories – use a low fat cream or curd cheese or quark (continental low fat cream cheese).

Utensils

Cook's knife; chopping board; bowl; teaspoon; fork

Ingredients

8 oz (225 g) any kind of cream
or cottage cheese (see above)
½ tsp salt
10 grinds black pepper

1 tsp finely cut chives
1 tsp finely chopped parsley
Pinch garlic salt
Pinch paprika

Method

1. Chop herbs finely.
2. Mix all the ingredients in the bowl using the fork.
3. Leave at room temperature for half an hour to allow the flavours to mature.
4. Serve with salad, or on crispbread, brown bread, digestive biscuits or toast.

Variation
As a dip for raw vegetables, add 3 tbsps yoghurt and a finely cut-up pickled cucumber to the mixture and mix thoroughly.

Yoghurt Plus

Natural yoghurt makes an instant satisfying and nutritious snack either by itself or with other ingredients. (If you eat a lot of yoghurt, you might consider investing in a yoghurt maker; follow the instructions, and you should be able to produce yoghurt at a third of the shop price.)

Variations

FRUIT YOGHURT

Additional Ingredient
1-2 tsps jam

Stir jam into yoghurt; it tastes just like expensive fruit yoghurt. (Also try adding honey.)

BREAKFAST YOGHURT
Pour on to a serving of muesli or crunch cereal instead of milk.

DESSERT YOGHURT

Additional Ingredients
Cut-up apples *or* pears *or* bananas
Sprinkle demerara sugar *or* ground hazelnuts *or* desiccated coconut

Pour yoghurt over fruit, and top with a sprinkle of sugar or nuts. (You can combine the alternatives!) You can also serve it with fruit jelly in place of cream.

SALAD DRESSING

Additional Ingredient
Mayonnaise

Mix equal quantities of mayonnaise and plain yoghurt together
for a lighter dressing for e.g. coleslaw.

RAITA

Additional Ingredients
4 in (10 cm) cucumber
1 spring onion
1 tsp fresh mint
1 tsp basil *or* parsley

Chop all ingredients finely, and mix with 2 small cartons natural
yoghurt. Use as an accompaniment to curry.

YOGHURT CREAM CHEESE
Makes 10 oz (275 g)
This is very soft and creamy, with a pleasing acidity. In the
Middle East it is known as 'Laban' or 'Labna'.

Utensils
Sieve; 2 light-coloured disposable kitchen cloths; basin

Method
1. Line sieve or strainer with double layer of clean light-coloured
   kitchen cloths and rest it on a basin.
2. Pour in 1 pint natural yoghurt, bring up ends of cloth to cover
   it lightly (for hygiene's sake), and leave in a cool place
   overnight or until all whey has dripped out.
3. Turn cheese into a basin. Either serve plain, or mix with finely
   chopped fruit (pineapple, banana, fresh peach, tangerine . . .)

Pan-Fried Steak

There may be an opportunity when you fancy spoiling yourself with a steak. You can grill a steak successfully on a domestic grill, but I prefer to pan-fry it, in an almost dry pan, or on a griddle – that's a cast-iron ridged utensil that gives steaks and chops the characteristic stripes that you usually associate with a charcoal grill. If you can acquire one somehow, do so, but they are expensive.

Utensils
Chopping board; cook's knife; paper towels; pastry brush (optional); heavy-based frying pan, or griddle; slotted spoon or spatula

Ingredients
2 steaks, each 6-8 oz (175-225 g)
Oil
4 tbsps dry red wine or strong

beef stock (made with a cube)
1 tsp Worcestershire sauce
Few grinds black pepper
$\frac{1}{2}$ tsp salt

Method
1. Put the steaks on the chopping board and nick through the outer fat layer at 1 in (2·5 cm) intervals (this stops the steak curling up at the edges and cooking unevenly).
2. Dry the steak thoroughly, using paper towels.
3. Pour in only enough oil to film the bottom of the pan (or if you've a pastry brush you can brush it on both sides of the meat instead).
4. Heat the pan for 4 minutes, until you can feel the heat on your hand held 3 in (7·5 cm) above the surface – test the heat by lowering the steak on to the pan. As the first corner touches the oil, it should sizzle encouragingly. If it merely makes a sad 'plop' wait a little longer. The first side should be richly brown in 4 minutes.
5. Remember that the cooking of a steak does not tenderize it; it merely browns the outside appetizingly and cooks the inside to the colour you prefer. Overcook a steak and it gets progressively tougher.
6. Turn the steak when it is browned, using a slotted spoon or spatula, rather than a knife which might pierce it and cause the juices to escape. After another 4 or 5 minutes, the steak should be 'à point' – that is pale pink inside and a rich brown outside.
7. *To test*, press it with your finger. It should resist slightly

instead of being soft like an uncooked steak. But to be sure, nick it with a knife and have a look.

8. Transfer the cooked steaks to a warm dish. Turn the heat down and add the remaining ingredients, stirring well to loosen any delicious drippings in the bottom of the pan, and also to concentrate the flavour (taste to be sure). Pour over the steak at once.

PAN-FRIED CHOPS (*Basic* recipe, p 110)

These are done in exactly the same way. However, I usually season the chops with Herbes de Provence, plenty of black pepper and a sprinkle of garlic salt 30 minutes before I intend to cook them. Most people like chops well cooked, so allow a good 10 minutes cooking time.

PAN-FRIED SAUSAGES (*Basic* recipe, p 110)

These are done in exactly the same way as the steak and chops but rather more slowly – the sausage needs to be cooked right through, but overheating will cause it to burst its skin.

13. Vegetables

There are many recipes containing vegetables in different chapters of the book. However, in this chapter we give our suggestions for cooking the most common varieties in the most straightforward way. Always remember that the more intense the colour of a vegetable – green, yellow, or purple – the fresher it is likely to be and the better the flavour and the higher the vitamin content. Dull, washed-out looking vegetables are usually stale and lacking in both taste and food value.

To cook frozen vegetables, follow the instructions on the packet; but remember the tip of heating butter until it is the colour of hazelnuts before mixing with the cooked vegetables.

Basic Cooking of Fresh Green Vegetables

To conserve their colour and food value, all green vegetables should be cooked as rapidly as possible in the minimum of boiling water, then eaten as soon as they are barely tender. (Sometimes, however, where cooker space is limited, it may be more convenient to steam them as several varieties can then be cooked at once.) The quantity given here will serve 4.

Utensils
Pan with lid; cook's knife; teaspoon; serrated-edge knife

Ingredients
1 lb (450 g) green vegetables
5 fl. oz (150 ml) water

1 tsp salt
Knob of butter

Method
1. Prepare the vegetables according to the variety (see below).
2. Bring the water to the boil with the salt.
3. Put in the prepared vegetables, bring the water back to the boil, cover and then boil rapidly for 8-10 minutes or until the vegetables feel barely tender when pierced with a slim knife.
4. Pour off the cooking water or strain in a colander.
5. Serve at once, plain or with a knob of butter which has been put in the pan and heated until it goes the colour of a hazelnut (it has much more flavour than uncooked butter).

SPROUTS

Choose tight, bright green sprouts. Remove any discoloured outer leaves and make sure there are no signs of maggots – if there are, discard the sprout. Make a little criss-cross nick in the stalk end to hasten the cooking, then leave in water to cover plus 1 teaspoon salt for half an hour. Rinse and cook as above.

CAULIFLOWER

Cut the flowerets from the stalk end, which you discard. Soak as above, then cook.

SPRING CABBAGE

Remove any coarse or discoloured outer leaves. Rinse the tender pale green inner leaves under the tap. Shred finely. Cook as above.

WHITE CABBAGE

Quarter and remove the white tough stalk section. Cut each quarter into shreds. Cook as above.

YOUNG GREEN CABBAGE

This is available in June and July. Quarter the cabbage head, then shred finely, discarding the stalk end. Half-fill a bowl with cold water and add 2 level tsps of salt. Put in the cabbage and leave for half an hour. Melt 2 oz (50 g) butter or margarine in the pan. Lift the cabbage from the water and put it into the hot fat, seasoning with black pepper. Cover and simmer in its own juices, shaking occasionally, until the cabbage is bite-tender (about 15 minutes). Uncover and shake over a low light to remove any excess moisture.

FRENCH OR RUNNER BEANS

Strip off the strings with a serrated-edge knife, rinse under the cold tap, cut in diagonal slices, or leave whole according to size. Cook as above.

BROAD BEANS

Shell and cook as above.

To Bake Potatoes

Utensils
Nylon pan scrub; potato peeler; fork; butter paper; oven tray

Ingredients
1 large potato per person   Salt

Method
1. Set the oven at Gas 6, 400°F, 200°C. Choose potatoes of an even size so they will all be ready at the same time.
2. Scrub thoroughly with a nylon pan scrub, then remove any eyes with the point of a potato peeler.
3. Dry thoroughly and prick all over with a fork (to stop the potato bursting).
4. Rub each potato with a butter or margarine paper to give it a light coating of fat.
5. Arrange well apart on a baking tray. Sprinkle lightly with salt to crispen the skin.
6. Bake for 1½ hours or until the potato feels tender when it is gently squeezed.

7. Remove from oven, and nick the skin on top, then squeeze the potato to break it and allow some of the steam to escape from inside. This makes the potato floury and light.
8. Serve at once with butter or sour cream or cottage cheese, salt and plenty of black pepper.

Chips for Two

The development of oven chips has taken much of the motivation away from learning the art of the chip frier. However, here is a quick method of cooking chips for 2 from scratch.

Utensils
Frying pan; potato peeler; cook's knife; mixing bowl; tea towel; slotted spoon; kitchen paper

Ingredients
2 large potatoes (¾ lb altogether)
Oil

Method
1. Put enough oil in the frying pan to come to depth of 1 in (2·5 cm).
2. Peel the potatoes, cut them into slices ⅜ in (9 mm) thick, then cut the slices into strips ⅜ in (9 mm) wide. Result: chips of equal width and depth (this is important for even cooking). (If you are great chip eaters you can, of course, invest in a chipper.)
3. Put the chips in cold water and leave for 10-15 minutes – this dissolves excess surface starch which would stop them becoming crisp.
4. Drain and dry thoroughly on a tea towel.
5. Heat the oil over a moderate light for about 5 minutes, or until a chip sizzles gently when it is put in.
6. Carefully put the remainder of the chips into the oil and cook at a steady but busy bubble for 7-10 minutes, or until they look a rich crisp brown.
7. Lift out with a slotted spoon, drain briefly on crumpled tissue or kitchen paper and serve at once.

Fried Potatoes for Two

These are often more convenient to cook for one or two people than roast potatoes or chips. The potatoes should be fried slowly at first, so as to absorb the fat, and then more quickly to crispen them just before serving. Cold leftover boiled potatoes can be used but you get the best results when the potatoes are actually cooked freshly in their skins.

Utensils
Panscrub; pan with lid; teaspoon; serrated-edge knife; frying pan; slotted spoon

Ingredients
1 lb (450 g) potatoes   1 tbsp oil
Salt   Black pepper
1 oz (25 g) butter or margarine

Method
1. Scrub the potatoes with the panscrub, then put them into the pan and cover with water. Add 2 tsps salt.
2. Bring the water slowly to the boil, then boil the potatoes for 25-40 minutes, according to size, until they feel quite tender when pierced with a sharp knife.
3. Drain the potatoes and return them to the empty pan to dry off on a low light (1-2 minutes).
4. Leave until cool enough to handle, then skin and cut into 1 in (2·5 cm) thick slices or cubes.
5. Put the fat in the pan and, when the butter or margarine starts to foam, lay in the potato slices and cook very gently, shaking the pan occasionally so that the potatoes absorb the fat rather than fry in it. This will take about 15 minutes.
6. When the potatoes are golden all over, increase the heat to make them crisp.
7. Drain from the fat (there should be very little left), put in a dish and sprinkle with salt and black pepper.

Perfect Mashed Potatoes for Two

Mashed potatoes are made fluffy by whisking over a low light with butter (or margarine) and hot milk or stock.

Utensils

Potato peeler; cook's knife; teaspoon; pan with lid; balloon whisk or large fork; tablespoon

Ingredients

1 lb (450 g) potatoes
1 tsp salt
1 tbsp (15 g) butter or margarine

4 tbsps hot milk (or chicken stock)

Method

1. Peel the potatoes, cut them in quarters and put them into the saucepan with salt.
2. Cover with cold water and bring to the boil, then cook at a steady boil for 15 minutes or until a potato feels absolutely tender when pierced with a sharp knife. (Don't boil the potatoes *too* vigorously or they may become 'soupy'.)
3. Take the pan to the sink, hold the lid at an angle to prevent the potatoes falling out, then drain off all the water.
4. Return to the cooker and leave on a low light until every drop of moisture has evaporated from the potatoes.
5. Pour the milk or chicken stock down the side of the pan and cut the butter or margarine in bits and place on top of the potatoes.
6. When the liquid is seen to be bubbling, beat it into the potatoes together with the fat, using a 'balloon' whisk or large fork.
7. Add a little more liquid if the potatoes seem to be too dry.
8. Continue to beat on a very low light until the mixture looks fluffy and creamy – about 3 minutes.
9. Taste and add more salt, if necessary, and the pepper.
10. Serve at once.

Aubergine Sauté
Serves 2

This is the best way to taste the characteristic flavour of this delicious vegetable in its simplest form, and a good recipe to serve with grilled or fried chops, beefburgers or steaks. Simply double the quantities to serve 4.

Utensils

Potato peeler; cook's knife; colander or sieve; plate and weight;

tea towel or kitchen paper; tablespoon; frying pan; teaspoon;
slotted spoon

Ingredients

1 large plump aubergine	1 tsp dried oregano
Salt	Sprinkle garlic salt
2 tbsps oil	5 grinds black pepper
2 tsps chopped parsley	

Method

1. Peel the aubergine, then cut into $\frac{1}{2}$ in (1·25 cm) cubes.
2. Put in a colander or sieve (or inside a salad spinner), sprinkle
   with salt, cover with a plate and something to weight it down,
   and leave for half an hour for the juices to drain away. (You
   can omit this stage but you will need twice as much oil to cook
   the aubergine.)
3. Rinse the aubergine with cold water, then dry either with a tea
   towel or kitchen paper or in the spinner.
4. Heat the oil in the frying pan until you can feel the heat on
   your hand held 2 in (5 cm) above it.
5. Put in the cubes and cook gently, shaking the pan occasionally
   until they are meltingly tender. After 10 minutes, add the
   garlic salt.
6. Lift out into a dish and sprinkle with the herbs and pepper.

NOTE: This dish can be reheated if required. It's also good served
cold with brown bread and butter.

Courgettes and Tomato Sauté
Serves 3-4 once or 1-2 twice

Courgettes can be sliced and fried like the aubergine (no need to
salt them), but we particularly like this method as it can also be
eaten cold.

Utensils
Cook's knife; chopping board; frying pan; slotted spoon;
tablespoon; teaspoon

Ingredients

1 lb (450 g) small courgettes
2 tbsps oil
3 large canned or fresh tomatoes

Sprinkle of garlic salt
½ tsp salt
10 grinds black pepper
1 tsp oregano

Method
1. Cut the courgettes in ¼ in (6 mm) thick slices.
2. Heat the oil in the pan until you can feel the heat on your hand held 2 in (5 cm) above the surface.
3. Put in the courgettes and cook gently, turning often until soft.
4. Now sprinkle with the garlic salt, add the tomatoes and cook gently together until thick but still juicy.
5. Season with salt, pepper and oregano.

COURGETTES NIÇOISE

Additional Ingredients

6 black olives   1 level tbsp chopped parsley

Stone and halve the olives, and add them and the parsley with the tomatoes at stage (4).

Peppers Sauté
Serves 2

Most people prefer the peppers with a little crispness in them, so cook only until a piece feels tender but firm when eaten. Simply double the ingredients to serve 4.

Utensils
Cook's knife; chopping board; frying pan; tablespoon; slotted spoon; teaspoon

Ingredients

2 glossy green or red peppers
1 tbsp salad oil
Pinch garlic salt

½ tsp Italian herbs
½ tsp salt
5 grinds black pepper

Method

1. Cut the peppers in half and remove the seeds and pith. Cut into strips, 3 to each half.
2. Heat the oil until you can feel the heat on your hand held 2 in (5 cm) above the pan, then add the peppers.
3. Cook quickly for a few minutes until they begin to soften, stirring frequently.
4. Sprinkle with the garlic salt, cover, lower the heat and allow to cook gently for a further 10 minutes.
5. Add the herbs, salt and pepper just before serving.

14. Salads and Their Dressings

There are two main kinds of salads – those that are ideal to accompany a 'main dish' of meat, fish, poultry, eggs or cheese, and those that are a meal in themselves. Both kinds of salad have one thing in common – they should have crispness somewhere in the ingredients. In addition, they should be dressed with, or be accompanied by, a dressing which complements their particular blend of flavours.

The crispness can be achieved in three ways: by cooking vegetable ingredients until they are just tender but with a little bite still left in them; by including an ingredient which is naturally crisp, such as celery or Chinese leaves; and by crispening the lettuce (or similar green stuff) – a job which really needs a salad spinner and a refrigerator.

A salad spinner costs about as much as a round of drinks and, in our opinion, is the only way to dry lettuce and similar greens. It acts on the principle of centrifugal force, an inner perforated basket spinning round and throwing the water out to the outer container. (It's not difficult to see why it also makes a good job of half-drying tights and smalls – after they have been washed, we hasten to add.)

Wash greens under the tap, put in the inner basket of the spinner and spin for 30 seconds. Lift out the greens, put in an old tea towel in the chosen salad bowl, then refrigerate until required. Very simple and very effective.

Dressings for Salads
Unless you insist, it really doesn't pay either from the point of view of time spent or money saved to make your own

mayonnaise, as there are excellent makes now on the market that compare very favourably with homemade. However, it is a good idea to have a stock of French dressing always to hand as this does not need refrigerating (any perishable ingredients such as herbs and onion can be added as needed for a particular salad).

Basic French Dressing
Enough for 12-14 servings of green salad in total

This dressing can be used for any kind of green salad.

Utensils
Screw-top jar; tablespoon; teaspoon

Ingredients

9 tbsps salad oil (corn, peanut, sunflower and if possible including 1-2 tbsps olive oil)
3 tbsps wine or cider vinegar *or* lemon juice

$\frac{1}{2}$ level tsp each salt and sugar
10 grinds black pepper
2 tsps English mustard (powder)

Method
1. Place all the ingredients in the screw-top jar and shake until it becomes a thick emulsion – about 2 minutes.
2. Use just enough to coat the greens in the salad.

Leftovers
Can be stored for weeks.

Variations

HERB FRENCH DRESSING

Add 2 level tbsps chopped mixed herbs – basil, parsley, chives, tarragon or any combination of two or more of them.

GARLIC FRENCH DRESSING

Leave a peeled clove of garlic in the amount of dressing you want to use for at least an hour. Discard before dressing the salad.

Basic Vinaigrette Dressing
Enough for 6-8 servings

This dressing is for *cooked* vegetable salads; it has a higher proportion of vinegar to salad oil, and is more highly seasoned.

Utensils
Screw-top jar; tablespoon; teaspoon; knife or garlic press; cook's knife; chopping board

Ingredients

4 tbsps any salad oil
2 tbsps wine vinegar
1 small clove garlic, crushed

1 level tsp salt
10 grinds black pepper
1 level tbsp chopped parsley

Method
1. Put all the ingredients into a screw-top jar and shake until thick – about 2 minutes.
2. Use just enough to coat the salad.

Variation

ONION VINAIGRETTE

Add 1 tbsp of chopped onion or snipped chives – or both!

Leftovers
Can be stored (even with herbs and onion) in the refrigerator for up to a week.

Salads to Accompany a Main Dish or as a Starter

Cyprus Tomato Salad
Serves 6 once, 2-3 twice

Utensils
Cook's knife; chopping board; serrated-edge knife; salad bowl

Ingredients

1 small or ½ large cucumber	Large sprig of parsley
4 large, ripe tomatoes	4 tbsps *Basic French Dressing*
1 large green pepper	

Method

1. Don't peel the cucumber unless the skin is very rough. Cut it and the tomatoes in ½ in (1·25 cm) cubes.
2. Halve the pepper, remove the seeds and white pith, then cut in ½ in (1·25 cm) squares.
3. Put into the chosen bowl together with the parsley divided into tiny sprigs.
4. Just before serving, sprinkle on the dressing and toss well.

Danish Cucumber Salad
Serves 6 once, 2-3 twice

This is more like a relish, very good with cold meat. The chives are vital for the final taste – and appearance.

Utensils
Potato peeler; cook's knife; soup plate; plate or saucer and weight; tablespoon; teaspoon; serving bowl

Ingredients

½ cucumber	1 tbsp boiling water
Salt	2 tbsps wine vinegar
Dressing	10 grinds black pepper
1 tbsp caster sugar	2 tsps finely cut chives

Method

1. Peel the cucumber, then slice it as thinly as you can into the soup plate. Sprinkle with salt, cover with an upturned saucer or plate and something to weight it down.
2. Leave for an hour – this removes excess water – then pour off the water.
3. To make the dressing, put the sugar in the serving bowl and pour on the boiling water, then stir until dissolved, and add all the remaining ingredients, including the cucumber.
4. Leave until cold before serving.

Coleslaw
Serves 6 once, 3 twice, 1 all week

We give this relatively large quantity as it isn't really worth making a smaller amount – and it keeps well in the refrigerator.

Utensils required
Cook's knife; chopping board; mixing bowl; potato peeler; grater; salad or serving bowl; tablespoon; teaspoon

Ingredients
1½ lb (700 g) white winter cabbage
1 large carrot
1 green pepper
2 oz (50 g) sultanas (optional)
1 oz peanuts or hazelnuts (optional)

Dressing
4 rounded tbsps mayonnaise
1 tbsp ordinary malt vinegar
1 tbsp caster sugar
1 tsp dry mustard

Method
1. Discard any discoloured leaves on the cabbage, quarter, then cut out the white core and discard.
2. Cut cabbage in shreds and put in the *mixing* bowl.
3. Peel and grate the carrot on top.
4. Halve the pepper, remove the white pith and seeds, then shred on top of the salad.
5. Add the sultanas and nuts (if used).
6. To make the dressing, put the mayonnaise in the salad bowl and simply stir in the remaining ingredients.
7. Add the salad ingredients from the mixing bowl and mix thoroughly so that the vegetables become coated with the dressing.
8. Leave for several hours in a cool place before serving.

Leftovers
Will keep two days in the larder, 5-6 days in the refrigerator.

Quick Coleslaw
Serves 4-5

Buy a 12 oz (350 g) carton of coleslaw and stir in some or all of the following: 1 small red apple, halved, cored and cut in little cubes; 2 sticks of celery, very thinly sliced; ½ small green pepper, cut in strips; and 1 heaped tbsp sultanas or raisins.

Carrot and Raisin Slaw
Serves 3-4

Cheap and easy: this salad can be just carrots and raisins in dressing. But if you feel ambitious you can add some hazelnuts – they make a terrific difference. We give a smaller amount than for coleslaw as carrots go soggy after a few days.

Utensils
Oven tray; tea towel; chopping board; cook's knife; tablespoon; teaspoon; salad bowl; potato peeler; grater

Ingredients
2 oz (50 g) hazelnuts or roasted peanuts
3 large carrots
3 tbsps raisins

Dressing
2 rounded tbsps mayonnaise or salad cream
Squeeze of lemon juice
1 tsp caster sugar

Method
1. If using hazelnuts, put them on the oven tray and place in the oven, preheated to Gas 5, 375°F, 190°C. Leave for about 10-15 minutes or until the skin begins to shrivel and the nuts look golden brown . . . don't worry if they suddenly get dark brown, as this slightly-burnt taste is delicious.
2. Take from the oven and put in a tea towel. Leave 5 minutes, then still wrapped in the tea towel, rub them together vigorously and the skins will come off.
3. Chop them coarsely with the knife. If peanuts are used, they don't need any treatment except chopping.
4. Put all the dressing ingredients into the salad bowl, mix together, then peel and grate the carrots on top.
5. Add the raisins and nuts and mix well.
6. Leave for at least 30 minutes before eating.

Celery and Apple Salad
Serves 3-4

Don't make too much of this as it really isn't nice after 2 days. But it's delicious when fresh.

Utensils
Cook's knife; chopping board; salad bowl; tablespoon; teaspoon

Ingredients
4 large stalks celery, cut in ¼ in (6 mm) slices
1 small red apple, halved, cored, cut in ½ in (1·25 cm) cubes
2 oz (50 g) fresh dates (optional but nice)
1 tbsp raisins

2 tbsps salted peanuts (optional)
Dressing
2 rounded tbsps mayonnaise
2 tsps each orange juice and lemon juice
Pinch brown sugar

Method
1. Put all the dressing ingredients into the salad bowl and stir to blend.
2. Add all the remaining ingredients – the celery, apple, and the dates (if used, stone and cut in 4 or 5 pieces), raisins and peanuts.
3. Mix thoroughly, then leave for at least half an hour before eating.

Beansprout Salad
Serves 3-4

A very easy but delicious salad – beansprouts are sold in many supermarkets.

Utensils
Cook's knife; chopping board; salad bowl; tablespoon

Ingredients
8 oz (225 g) or carton of beansprouts
2 tbsps raisins or sultanas
Smallest packet dry roasted peanuts

1 red pepper, chopped finely
3 tbsps soy sauce
Pinch salt
5 grinds black pepper

Method
1. Put all the ingredients into the salad bowl and mix well.
2. Leave in cool place for 1 hour before serving.

Main Dish Salads

These salads will all provide a main dish, be it light or substantial, as they all contain some form of protein.

Caroline's Cambridge Salad
Serves 2 (more if with other dishes)

Utensils
Salad bowl; tablespoon; teaspoon; potato peeler; grater; chopping board; cook's knife

Ingredients

2 carrots	*Dressing*
1 crisp apple	1 tbsp mayonnaise
1 banana	1 tbsp orange juice
2 tbsp seedless raisins	2 tsps lemon juice
Very small packet peanuts	$\frac{1}{2}$ tsp salt
1 tbsp porage oats	

Method
1. Put all the dressing ingredients into the salad bowl and stir to blend.
2. Peel, then grate the carrots; halve, core and coarsely chop the apple; peel and slice banana quite thickly.
3. Add these, together with the raisins, peanuts and oats to the dressing and stir well.
4. Leave for half an hour before eating.

Leftovers
Don't leave any, as banana will go soggy.

Greek Salad
Serves 3-4

This is a green salad converted into a main dish by some cheese.

Utensils

Salad spinner; serrated-edge knife; chopping board; salad bowl; tablespoon, teaspoon; screw-top jar for dressing

Ingredients

1 crisp lettuce of any kind
1 bunch watercress
4 in (10 cm) section of cucumber
½ lb (225 g) firm tomatoes
Large sprig of parsley
6 oz crumbly Lancashire or Cheshire cheese (*haloumi* is the one used in Greece and Cyprus)

2 oz (50 g) black olives (optional but authentic, particularly if they are the variety known as 'calamata')

Dressing

Use ½ quantity of *Basic French Dressing* (p 122); add clove of garlic

Method

1. Earlier in the day wash the lettuce and dry in a spinner (without one, dab dry with tea towel). Cover and leave in the refrigerator.
2. At the same time, rinse the watercress under the tap, then cut off the tough stalks and discard. Dry the leaves, and put in the refrigerator.
3. Shortly before eating, peel the cucumber (if skin is tough) and cut in ½ in (1·25 cm) cubes. Do the same with the tomatoes.
4. Tear the lettuce into bite-size pieces and mix with the watercress in the salad bowl.
5. Arrange the cucumber and tomato cubes, the cheese (cut in ½ in or 1·25 cm cubes), the parsley, divided into tiny flowerets, and the olives on top.
6. Toss with the dressing at the table.

Salade Niçoise

Serves 3-4

To get the true Niçoise flavour, try and obtain fresh herbs for the dressing.

Utensils

Cook's knife; serrated-edge knife; chopping board; small bowl; salad bowl; screw-top jar; tablespoon; teaspoon for dressing; small pan; fork; can opener

Ingredients

3 firm tomatoes
½ medium cucumber
Bunch of spring onions
4 in (10 cm) section of Chinese leaves *or* small crisp lettuce (Webb or Iceberg)

1 7oz (200 g) can tuna
2 eggs
1 small can flat anchovies (optional)
2 oz (50 g) stuffed green or black olives

Half quantity *Basic Vinaigrette Dressing* with 1 tbsp each chopped parsley and chives

Method

1. Prepare *Basic Vinaigrette Dressing* (see p 123), adding chopped parsley and chives.
2. Quarter tomatoes and remove seeds if very juicy.
3. Cut the cucumber in ½ in (1·25 cm) chunks.
4. Halve the pepper, remove the white pith and seeds, and slice thinly.
5. Cut off roots and discoloured leaves of spring onions, then slice in ½ in (1·25 cm) sections.
6. Put all prepared vegetables into the small bowl, and mix with half the dressing.
7. Cut Chinese leaves or lettuce into very fine shreds, then put in salad bowl and arrange the tomatoes, cucumbers, pepper and spring onions on top. Leave in a cool place for at least half an hour.
8. Meanwhile, prepare hard-boiled eggs (see p 40).
9. Just before serving, decorate salad with the tuna (drained and divided into large flakes), halved hard-boiled eggs, drained anchovies and sliced olives.
10. At the table, mix all gently together and serve with the remaining dressing.

Leftovers

The salad will go soggy, so do not leave any.

Tuna Salad
Serves 2-3

Utensils

Can opener; fork; cook's knife; serrated-edge knife; chopping board; salad bowl; screw-top jar; tablespoon; teaspoon

Ingredients

1 × 7 oz (200 g) can tuna
3 in (7·5 cm) fresh cucumber
or 1 large pickled cucumber
2 firm tomatoes
½ onion
Dressing
1 tbsp mayonnaise

1 tbsp *Basic Vinaigrette
Dressing* (see p 123)
10 grinds black pepper
½ tsp salt
Squeeze lemon juice
Pinch nutmeg
1 tsp fresh chopped parsley or
chives

Method

1. Drain the tuna and flake with the fork.
2. Cut the cucumber and tomato in tiny cubes, and chop the
   onion finely.
3. Put all into the salad bowl.
4. Put all the dressing ingredients into the screw-top jar and
   shake until blended.
5. Gently mix with the tuna and vegetables. Leave 30 minutes
   before eating.

Leftovers

Will keep one day in the larder, 3 days in the refrigerator.

Tuna and Rice Salad
Serves 4-5

A heartier, more filling salad.

Utensils

Small lidded pan; teaspoon; can opener; fork; chopping board;
cook's knife; salad bowl

Ingredients

16 fl oz (450 ml) water
½ tsp salt
7 oz (200 g) Italian or long-
grain rice
1 7 oz (200 g) can tuna

1 medium onion, finely
chopped
2 tbsps *Basic Vinaigrette
Dressing* (see p 123)

Method

1. Bring water to the boil with the salt. Add the rice, stir well,
   bring back to boiling point, then reduce to a simmer, cover

and cook until the water has been absorbed and rice is in separate grains (about 20 minutes).
2. Meanwhile, drain tuna and divide into large flakes with the fork, and chop onion.
3. Add tuna and onion to rice.
4. Stir in the *Basic Vinaigrette Dressing* and allow to go cold before serving.

Leftovers
Will keep 1 day in the larder, 3 days in the refrigerator.

Rice and Pepper Salad
Serves 4-5

Utensils
Small lidded saucepan; tablespoon; teaspoon; serrated-edge knife; chopping board; salad bowl

Ingredients

16 fl. oz (450 ml) water	2 tbsps raisins or sultanas
½ tsp salt	3 tbsps grated or cubed hard
10 grinds black pepper	cheese (Cheddar, Lancashire
Pinch ground nutmeg	etc)
7 oz (200 g) Italian or long-	2 tbsps *Basic Vinaigrette*
grain rice	*Dressing* (see p 123)
1 red or green pepper	

Method
1. Bring water to the boil in the pan, with the salt, pepper and nutmeg.
2. Add the rice, bring back to the boil, then reduce to a simmer; cover and cook for 20 minutes or until water has been absorbed and rice grains are separate.
3. Meanwhile, halve the pepper, remove the seeds and white pith, then divide into ½ in (1·25 cm) squares.
4. When the rice is cooked add pepper, raisins or sultanas, cheese and dressing.
5. Stir well and leave until cold before eating.

Leftovers
Keep 1 day in larder, 3 days in the refrigerator.

Variation

SUMMER RICE SALAD

Additional Ingredients
4 oz (125 g) button mushrooms, sliced wafer thin.
Omit cheese from *Rice and Pepper Salad* recipe.

15. Rice and Pasta

Rice

Until about twenty years ago, most rice came in hessian sacks, with a full quota of stones, dirt and rubbish. The cooking quality of the rice also varied from one country to another, and indeed from one crop to the next, so a major part of the preparation of rice for cooking used to be in the cleansing, whilst the cooking process itself had to be varied according to its quality and country of origin.

Today it is a very different story. Most of the rice sold in the Western world is pre-cleaned and packeted. The quality is standardized and so therefore is the cooking method.

But every country that grows rice has its own way of cooking it. We have tried many of these methods and if the rice is of good quality they seem to work equally well. However, the easiest and most consistently successful way seems to be the *pilaff* method: the rice is first fried in fat – sometimes with a little onion – and then cooked without stirring in a measured amount of water or stock (made with a stock cube). If a good quality Italian, American, Basmati or brown rice is cooked in this way, it will always give a good result, with the rice fluffy or creamy according to its type. A simpler method is to wash it thoroughly to remove the outer coating of starch which might make it sticky, then boil it without frying in a measured amount of water or stock. (The washing can be omitted if parboiled packeted rice is used.)

American parboiled rice (e.g. 'Uncle Ben's') is an excellent general purpose rice and gives the largest yield if cooked according to the pack instructions. *Basmati* rice (from Pakistan) can be bought loose or in packets. It is, as you would expect, ideal for curries. *Italian* rice is creamier when cooked and is excellent for making a risotto. *Brown* rice has a delicious nutty flavour and chewy texture and is especially nutritious but it takes at least twice the length of time to cook as other kinds of rice. *Shortgrain* rice is the one used for sweet rice puddings as it becomes very soft and creamy when cooked slowly in the oven.

For *Vegetable Risotto*, see p 140, and for rice salads see pp 131-3.

Storing cooked rice
As rice will keep up to a week in a covered container in the refrigerator, it's a good idea to make up a large quantity so that it can be included in several meals – for instance by adding it to soup, making a salad, serving 'as is' or making into a main dish risotto.

NOTE: If you cook a large quantity of rice in advance, cool it as quickly as possible by spreading on a tray, then refrigerate. This avoids the slight risk of food poisoning.

Reheating rice
Cover the bottom of a pan or ovenproof casserole to a depth of $\frac{1}{4}$ in (6 mm) with boiling water or stock (made with a chicken, beef or vegetable cube), then add the rice. Cover and reheat, either top of stove over moderate heat until steaming (stirring occasionally with a fork, not a spoon which packs the rice together), or for 15 minutes in the oven at Gas 4, 350°F, 180°C.

Quantities
Allow $1\frac{1}{2}$-2 oz (40-50 g or 3-4 tbsps) raw rice per serving as an accompaniment.
For a salad allow 1 oz (25 g or 2 tbsps) raw rice per serving.
Allow $2\frac{1}{2}$ oz (65 g or 5 tbsps) raw rice per serving as a main dish.

To measure
A large teacup (8 fl oz) holds 7 oz raw rice – enough for 4 helpings. We would always recommend that you use a cup or measuring jug to measure the amount of rice and water. It's very much easier than weighing everything out; and if you use the same measure for rice and liquid the proportions will be right.

Basic Boiled Rice

Serves 4 once, 2 twice, 1 four times
This is to serve in place of potatoes with curries and other
savoury dishes.

Utensils
Lidded saucepan with a heavy base; a cup or liquid measure;
tablespoon; teaspoon

Ingredients
1 cup (7 oz or 200 g) packeted
parboiled long-grain rice
2½ cups (1 pint or 575 ml)
water

1 oz (25 g) butter or margarine
or 2 tbsps oil
1 level tsp salt

Method
1. Put all the ingredients into the pan. Bring to the boil, stir once
   then reduce to a simmering point on a low light.
2. Cover and cook for 15-20 minutes without stirring.
3. Uncover and fluff up with a fork – the rice will be cooked but
   still separate.

NOTE: If using long-grain rice that has not been parboiled, use
only 2 cups (¾ pint or 425 ml) liquid.

Variations

RICHER BOILED RICE

Additional Ingredients
2 Beef, Chicken or Vegetable stock cubes.

Put the cubes in the pan, pour on the water and bring to the boil,
stirring to dissolve the cubes. Add the remaining ingredients and
cook as for *Basic Boiled Rice*.

FRIED RICE ITALIAN STYLE (*Basic* recipe, above)
Serves 2-3

A quick and tasty 'fry-up', using leftover cooked rice. You need
approximately 2 cups of cooked rice.

Utensils
Large frying pan or saucepan; fork; tablespoon; teaspoon

Additional Ingredients
2 oz (50 g) butter or margarine
1 tsp salt
Speck white pepper and
nutmeg

2 tbsps grated Parmesan cheese
Additional butter and cheese
on the table

Method
1. Melt the butter in the pan over moderate heat, then add the rice and stir it with a fork so that it absorbs the butter and is reheated at the same time.
2. Add the salt, pepper and nutmeg together with the cheese.
3. Serve piping hot, and let each person stir in extra butter and Parmesan cheese to their own taste.

FRIED RICE, CHINESE STYLE (*Basic* recipe, p 136)
Serves 4

This can either be made with leftover *Basic Boiled Rice* or the rice can be cooked freshly. You need approximately 3 cups of cooked rice, 1 cup (7 oz or 200 g) raw.

Utensils required
Cook's knife; chopping board; frying pan; tablespoon; teaspoon

Additional Ingredients
1 onion *or* 1 tbsp onion flakes
1 green or red pepper *or* 1 tbsp
pepper flakes
¼ lb (125 g) mushrooms
2 tbsps oil *or* 1 oz (25 g) butter

1 tsp salt
10 grinds black pepper
1 tbsp soy sauce
1 tbsp chopped (or 2 tsps dried)
parsley

Method
1. If fresh onions and peppers are used, peel, de-seed the peppers, then chop or cut up coarsely. Thinly slice the mushrooms.
2. Heat the fat until it melts or you can feel the heat of the pan on your hand held 2 in (5 cm) above the surface. Add the chopped onion and green pepper (if used) and the mushrooms and fry in the fat until the onion becomes golden brown. The

fresh pepper should still be crisp (taste a bit to see).

3. Now add the rice, the pepper and onion flakes (if used), the salt, pepper, soy sauce and herbs.
4. Fry gently, stirring constantly with a fork until the rice is steaming hot. Serve at once.

Basic Savoury Rice
Serves 4 once, 2 twice, 1 four times

In this method, the rice is first lightly fried with chopped onion and then simmered in liquid until it is cooked. It is rather more trouble to make than Basic Boiled Rice, but it is also rather more tasty, particularly as the basis of a pilaff.

Utensils
Cook's knife; chopping board; tablespoon; lidded saucepan with heavy base

Ingredients

1 medium onion *or* 1 tbsp onion flakes
2 tbsps oil *or* 1 oz (25 g) butter or margarine
1 cup (7 oz or 200 g) any kind of long-grain or Basmati rice
2 cups (16 fl oz or 450 ml) hot stock made with a chicken or vegetable cube

2 tsps salt
15 grinds black pepper
1 tsp paprika (optional)
2 tsps tomato purée (optional)
Pinch garlic salt (optional)

Method
1. Peel, then chop the onion finely.
2. Heat the oil or chosen fat for 2-3 minutes or until you can feel the heat of the pan on your hand held 2 in (5 cm) above the surface of the pan.
3. Add the fresh onion (if used) then cook for 5 minutes over moderate heat until softened and golden. (You don't need to cook onion flakes.)
4. Add the rice (well rinsed if not packeted)and turn in the onion over moderate heat for 3 minutes.
5. Add the hot stock, salt and pepper (and the onion flakes, paprika, tomato purée and garlic salt, if used) and stir well.

6. Bring to the boil, then cover and cook for 20 minutes over a low heat, either on top of the stove or in the oven at Gas 6, 400°F, 200°C (whichever is the most convenient).

Leftovers
Will keep for 1 week covered under refrigeration. Not more than 1 day in a cool larder.

Variations

SAVOURY BROWN RICE

Cook as for *Basic Savoury Rice* but boil for 20 minutes, then turn the heat as low as possible and allow to cook (covered) for another 30 minutes, on top of the stove or in a moderate oven (Gas 4, 350°F, 180°C).

RICE COOKED INDIAN STYLE

This is a useful technique if there is no way of measuring the liquid.

Additional Utensil
Tea towel

Method
1. Fry the onion and add the rice as in the recipe for *Basic Savoury Rice*, opposite.
2. After the rice has been turned in the fat for 3 minutes, cover with cold water or stock to come 1 in (2·5 cm) above the surface of the rice.
3. Bring to the boil, then cover the pan with a tea towel and then a lid (making sure the tea towel doesn't touch the gas or electric element).
4. Simmer for 20 minutes by which time the rice should have absorbed all the liquid.

LIVER RISOTTO (*Basic* recipe, p 138)
Serves 3-4
Use any long grain rice

Additional Ingredients

2 oz (50 g) mushrooms
½ lb (225 g) chicken or lamb's
liver (washed and drained)
1 clove of garlic or pinch of
garlic salt

4 fl oz (125 ml) left-over red
or white wine (optional)
1 rounded tbsp tomato purée *or*
8 oz (225 g) can tomatoes
2 tsps brown sugar

Method

1. Slice the mushrooms; halve the chicken livers or cut the
   lamb's liver into little cubes.
2. Cook as directed for *Basic Savoury Rice*, but fry the liver,
   mushrooms and garlic with the onion until golden brown, and
   add the wine (if used), the tomato purée and sugar with the
   stock.
3. Bring the risotto to the boil, cover and cook over low heat for
   20 minutes top of stove or in the oven at Gas 6, 400°F,
   200°C, whichever is most convenient.

ALL IN ONE RISOTTO (*Basic* recipe, p 138)
Serves 2-3

An excellent store cupboard main dish when you can't think what
to eat. Serve hot; though it is also delicious eaten cold. Use
Italian risotto rice.

Additional Ingredients

2 tbsps frozen peas or any
leftover vegetables
1 tsp tomato purée
2 tsps soy sauce

½ tsp sugar
Pinch nutmeg
1 tbsp grated Parmesan cheese

Method

1. Cook the *Basic Savoury Rice* as directed. After 10 minutes, add
   the frozen peas if used.
2. When the rice is ready, stir in all the remaining ingredients
   with a fork.
3. Heat 2-3 minutes, then serve piping hot with more Parmesan
   or other grated cheese.

SAUSAGE RISOTTO (*Basic* recipe, p 138)
Serves 2-3
Use either fried ordinary sausages, parboiled Viennas or
Frankfurters.

Additional Ingredients
½-¾ lb cooked sausages

Method
1. Prepare the *Basic Savoury Rice* as directed.
2. While it is cooking, cut the sausages into ½ in (1·25 cm) slices
3. After 10 minutes cooking of the rice, add sausages and cook
   for a further 10 minutes.

KOREAN RICE (*Basic* recipe, p 138)
Serves 3-4

Additional Ingredients
3 tbsps sesame seeds (optional, but delicious)
½ lb (225 g) raw minced meat
2-4 oz (50-125 g) mushrooms
1 tbsp soy sauce

Method
1. Put the sesame seeds into the pan in which you intend to cook
   the rice, and toast them over a moderate heat for 3-4 minutes
   until the seeds are golden. Remove from the pan; put them in
   a saucer until you need them.
2. Now make the *Basic Savoury Rice* as directed, but brown the
   meat and mushrooms with the onion before adding the rice.
3. When the meat has lost its redness, add all the remaining *Basic
   Savoury Rice* ingredients and stir well.
4. Bring to the boil, reduce to a simmer and cook for 20 minutes
   either on top of the stove or in the oven at Gas 6, 400°F,
   200°C for 20 minutes.
5. Just before serving, stir in the soy sauce and the toasted
   sesame seeds.

Creamy Rice For One

A filling lunch on a cold day.

Utensils required
Pan with lid; cook's knife; chopping board; large cup or liquid measure; small bowl; fork; tablespoon; teaspoon

Ingredients
½ oz (15 g) butter
½ medium onion
½ cup (3½ oz or 90 g) Italian risotto rice
1 cup (8 fl oz or 225 ml) water

½ tsp salt
Pinch white pepper
Pinch grated nutmeg
1 egg
1 tbsp grated Parmesan cheese

Method
1. Melt the butter and add the onion. Cover and steam through for 3 minutes.
2. Uncover, add rice and fry gently for 2 minutes.
3. Add water, salt, pepper and nutmeg. Bring to the boil, then cover.
4. Simmer 15 minutes until all the water has been absorbed but the rice still looks a little wet.
5. Beat the egg in the bowl, then add to rice, stirring constantly over gentle heat (don't *over*cook as you want the mixture to be creamy, not with bits of cooked egg).
6. Serve sprinkled with the grated cheese.

NOTE: This can be varied by adding sliced mushrooms or peppers and frying with the onion at the beginning. It could be made with 1 cup leftover rice (*Basic Boiled* or *Basic Savoury*), simply heating it through with all the other ingredients.

Pasta

The best pasta is made from durum semolina – that is, winter wheat which has a high protein (gluten) content. If it is made from soft (low gluten) wheat, it is very starchy and tends to become sloppy when cooked. Excellent pasta of all kinds, both with and without eggs, is imported from Italy and there is also a thriving British pasta industry. Let your palate be your guide as to which you choose.

Pasta is rather like rice in that it is an excellent 'host' for all kinds of sauces and mixtures, and will make a little meat go a long way.

It also makes an excellent cheap snack, simply boiled, then tossed with plenty of butter and cheese in the Italian fashion. Noodles of different widths make very good soup garnishes, and are delicious with Chinese stir-fry dishes (see pp 90-97).

However, whatever variety of pasta you use, it must be cooked in plenty of water and only until the stage called 'al dente' – that is, when you chew a piece it should feel soft but with a little bite still left.

Basic Method of Cooking Spaghetti
Serves 4-5

Utensils
Your largest pan (if possible, 6 pint or 3·5 l capacity); sieve or colander; 2 tablespoons; teaspoon

Ingredients

1 lb (500 g) durum wheat spaghetti
Salt
1 tbsp vegetable oil

Further 1-2 tbsps oil (preferably olive)
10 grinds black pepper

Method
1. Fill the pan two-thirds full of water, add 4 heaped tsps salt and bring to the boil.
2. When the water is bubbling fiercely, add the tablespoon of vegetable oil, then gently lower in the spaghetti, allowing it to coil inside the pan as it softens (don't break it).
3. Cook with the lid partially on (which stops it boiling over) at a fierce bubble for 12 minutes, then bite a piece.
4. If it feels soft but still with a little bite left, it is ready! Otherwise, give it a couple more minutes before testing again.
5. As soon as it is cooked to your satisfaction, take to the sink, add a splash of cold water so that it stops cooking, then drain, preferably through a sieve or a colander (otherwise tilt the lid carefully so that the water goes out but not the pasta). Add the remaining 1-2 tablespoons of oil together with a further sprinkle of salt and the 10 grinds black pepper.
6. Toss with two spoons until each strand of spaghetti is gleaming with the oil.

7. Serve plain with butter and grated cheese, or use as an accompaniment to *Bolognese Sauce* (see p 74) or *Chicken Liver Sauce* (see p 76).

Basic Method of Cooking Noodles and Short Cut Macaroni
Serves 4 once or 2 twice

These are much easier to cook, as they are easier to handle and don't need so much water. We prefer them cooked until quite tender (though not sloppy).

Utensils
Medium lidded pan; colander or sieve; tablespoon; teaspoon

Ingredients
½ lb (225 g) broad egg noodles   Salt and pepper to taste
or short cut macaroni

Method
1. Look at the packet as cooking times vary. Indeed, some makes of Chinese-style noodles don't need cooking at all – you simply cover them with boiling water and leave for a given time, usually about 8 minutes.
2. If they do need cooking, half-fill the pan with water, add 1 tsp salt. Bring to the boil.
3. Add the noodles or macaroni, bring back to the boil and boil with the lid partly on for 8 minutes or until they feel quite tender when one is tasted.
4. Drain through the colander or sieve, or by tilting the lid of the pan.
5. The pasta is now ready to be mixed with other ingredients (see *Macaroni Cheese*, p 53, *Tuna and Macaroni*, p 54) or served plain instead of potatoes or rice to accompany a main dish.

NOTE: Fine noodles (or vermicelli) make an excellent soup garnish and can be cooked in the soup itself for 5 minutes.

Leftovers
Keep covered 4 days in the refrigerator, 2 days in a larder cupboard.

PARSLEYED NOODLES
Serves 4-5

This is a particularly delicious way of serving them either as an accompaniment or – with the addition of cheese – as a main dish.

Additional Ingredients
Stock made with chicken or vegetable bouillon cube
2 oz (50 g) butter or margarine
2 tbsps chopped parsley
15 grinds black pepper
Salt
4 tbsps Parmesan cheese (optional)

Method
1. Cook the noodles as in basic method but using stock instead of water.
2. Put in sieve or colander and pour cold water through to remove any excess starch. Drain well.
3. In the pan in which the noodles were cooked, melt the fat, add the parsley. Add the drained noodles and toss well to coat in the parsley and fat, adding black pepper and salt to taste.
4. Serve steaming hot, plain or scattered with the cheese.

16. Pastry Quiches and Fruit Pies

Quiches (or savoury flans) and fruit pies are very simple to make, except for just one thing – mixing and rolling out the pastry. If you are anxious to learn how to handle pastry, it's a good idea to go and watch someone doing just that – it's very difficult to describe in words, as so much depends on feeling the texture of the pastry and watching the technique of rolling out.

However, if you don't want to make your own pastry, you have several options. You can buy quiche shells ready-to-fill from a local baker (many of whom now provide this service), or you can make them from fat, ground nuts and breadcrumbs as we describe below (very delicious but, of course, not quite as crisp as regular pastry). And you can also make quiche shells from ready-to-roll shortcrust pastry.

So, although we will give you detailed instructions on preparing the pastry from scratch, do use the options if you haven't the time or the skill to do so.

The Quiche or Savoury Flan

The French quiche is first cousin to the British savoury flan. However, the quiche is usually filled with a savoury *custard* and the flan is made with a savoury *sauce*. In our recipes we have combined the best features of both these methods by adding a little cornflour to the eggs and cream. This kind of filling has more body than a quiche and is lighter in texture than a flan.

If the case is baked 'blind' (empty), it will not go soggy when the filling is added. However, if this is too much hassle, you can bake the case and the filling together, standing it on an *oven tray* which has been heated up with the oven.

NOTE: Quiches should be served warm or at room temperature, but never hot. Unless otherwise stated, they may be reheated in a moderate oven (Gas 4, 350°F, 180°C for 20 minutes or until warm to the touch). Quiches can be made in loose-bottomed metal quiche cases or in ones made of ovenproof pottery.

Leftovers
Keep for 1 day in the larder, 3 days in the refrigerator.

Quiche Pastry Case
Makes 1 shallow 10 in (25 cm) case or 1 deeper 8 in (20 cm) one.

Utensils
Sieve; mixing bowl; knife; cup or jug; film or foil; rolling pin; pastry board or plastic table top or counter; flan case; fork

Ingredients

5 oz (150 g) plain flour
Pinch of salt
1 level tsp icing sugar

3 oz (75 g) firm butter or block margarine
2-3 tbsps ice-cold water

Method
1. Sift the flour, salt and icing sugar into the mixing bowl and stir well to mix thoroughly.
2. Cut the fat into 1 in chunks, then add to the dry ingredients and rub into them between the fingers and thumb of each hand until each particle of fat is the size of a small pea.
3. Sprinkle with the water to moisten the dry ingredients evenly so that they can be gathered into a dough, first with your fingers and then the whole hand. The dough should be moist enough to hold together without being sticky (add a little more water if necessary).
4. Wrap the dough in film or foil and put in a cool place for 1 hour – this helps to make it easier to roll out and stops the dough shrinking in the oven.
5. Sprinkle clean worktop or pastry board lightly with flour, sprinkle rolling pin with flour and roll pastry out to fit the chosen flan case; trim it even with the top rim of the dish.

6. Prick all over the bottom and sides with a fork – this stops it bubbling up. (If you don't want to bake it blind it is now ready to fill, but do remember to heat the oven tray first.)
7. To bake it blind, press a piece of foil into the shape of the inside of the quiche case so that the pastry is completely covered, particularly at the edges. If possible, chill (or, even better, freeze) for 30 minutes.
8. Bake at Gas 7, 425°F, 215°C for 10 minutes or until the pastry is set and firm to the touch; then remove the foil, prick the base with the fork yet again, turn heat down to Gas 5, 375°F, 190°C, and continue to bake for a further 12-15 minutes, until quite dry to the touch but only faintly coloured. It is now ready for filling.

No-roll Nutty Breadcrumb Quiche Case

Utensils
Bowl; fork; quiche or flan dish

Ingredients
5 oz (150 g) wholewheat bread (about 7 large slices)

4 oz (125 g) soft butter or margarine
2 oz (50 g) ground hazelnuts

Method
1. Crumb the bread with a fork.
2. Put the soft fat into a bowl, add the crumbs and nuts, squeeze and knead together until the mixture forms a ball.
3. Grease the chosen quiche dish, then work the pastry over the bottom and sides.
4. Chill for 30 minutes. It is now ready to fill.

NOTE: If you can't find ground hazelnuts, or just don't like them, you can use another 3 slices of bread instead.

Basic Mushroom Quiche
Serves 4

Utensils
Cook's knife; chopping board; frying pan; teaspoon; tablespoon; bowl; batter whisk; grater

Ingredients
1 baked, unbaked or breadcrumb case (see p 148)

Mushroom mixture
¼ onion or 4 spring onions	5 fl oz (150 ml) single cream
1 oz (25 g) butter	or one 6 oz (175 g) can
¼ lb (125 g) mushrooms	evaporated milk
1 tsp salt	Pinch each salt and nutmeg
1 tsp lemon juice	5 grinds black pepper
1 tbsp sweet sherry	*Topping*
Savoury custard	1 oz (25 g or 3 tbsps) grated
1 tbsp cornflour	Cheddar cheese
2 large eggs (size 2 or 3)	Nut of butter

Method
1. Finely chop the onion or slice the spring onions.
2. Melt the butter in the frying pan, add the onion and cook for 2 minutes then add the mushrooms (sliced ¼ in or 6 mm thick), the salt, lemon juice and sherry.
3. Cover and cook gently for 5 minutes, uncover and cook briskly until all the liquid has evaporated and the mushrooms are beginning to fry in the butter. Remove from heat.
4. Now make the savoury custard: put the cornflour in the bowl, add the cream or evaporated milk slowly whisking, then add the eggs and seasonings and whisk together until just smooth.
5. Add the mushroom mixture to the savoury custard, then pour into the quiche case.
6. Scatter with the grated cheese and dot with tiny bits of butter.
7. Bake at Gas 5, 375°F, 190°C for 25 minutes, then at Gas 4, 350°F, 180°C for 10 minutes, or until golden brown and puffed. The flan will remain puffed for 30 minutes.
8. Allow to rest for at least 10 minutes as it is nicer warm rather than hot.

Variations

TUNA OR SALMON QUICHE (*Basic* recipe, p 148)
Serves 4

This needs a baked, unbaked or breadcrumb case (see p 148), and the savoury custard from *Basic Mushroom Quiche*.

Utensils

As for *Basic Mushroom Quiche* with extra bowl and fork. No frying pan.

Additional Ingredients

7 oz (200 g) can tuna or pink salmon

1 tbsp snipped fresh chives, dill

or parsley, *or* 1 tsp dried herbs

4 oz grated sharp cheese

½ tsp Worcestershire sauce

Omit Mushroom mixture from *Basic Mushroom Quiche* recipe

Method

1. Make case.
2. Make the savoury custard.
3. Drain the fish, flake with a fork, then add to the savoury custard, together with the herbs, all the cheese except 1 tbsp, and Worcestershire sauce.
4. Pour gently into the quiche case, sprinkle with the remaining grated cheese and nut of butter.
5. Bake in a moderate oven (Gas 5, 375°F, 190°C) for 25 minutes, then turn down (to Gas 4, 350°F, 180°C) and bake for a further 10 minutes or until puffed and golden brown.
6. Cool 10 minutes before serving.

CHEESE AND OLIVE QUICHE (*Basic* recipe, p 148)
Serves 4

This needs a baked, unbaked or breadcrumb case (see p 148), and the savoury custard from *Basic Mushroom Quiche*.

Utensils

As for *Basic Mushroom Quiche*; no frying pan

Additional Ingredients

4 oz (125 g) grated cheese (such as Cheddar or Lancashire)

2 tsps snipped chives

2 oz (50 g) sliced stuffed olives

1 tsp Dijon or English made mustard

Omit Mushroom mixture from *Basic Mushroom Quiche* recipe

Method
1. Make case.
2. Make the savoury custard.
3. Add to the custard all the additional ingredients, mixing well.
4. Pour into the flan case and bake at Gas 5, 375°F, 190°C for 25 minutes, then at Gas 4, 350°F, 180°C for 10 minutes, or until puffed and golden brown.
5. Serve warm or cold.

Cream Cheese Quiche
Serves 4

This is a speciality of the Alsace region of France. It is a slightly different mixture – and has a different texture from the preceding quiches.

Utensils
Oven tray; cook's knife; chopping board; teaspoon; tablespoon; bowl; batter whisk; grater

Ingredients
4 oz (125 g) full fat cream cheese

1 oz (25 g) grated sharp cheese (Lancashire or Cheddar)

4 fl oz (125 ml) single cream or evaporated milk

2 eggs (size 3 or 4)

2 tsps each snipped chives and chopped parsley

½ tsp grated lemon rind

8 grinds of black pepper

1 quiche case of any kind

Topping

1 oz (25 g) grated Cheddar cheese

Nut of butter

Method
1. Put an empty tray in the oven, set at Gas 6, 400°F, 200°C.
2. Put the two cheeses into a bowl, then gradually add first the cream (or evaporated milk) and then all the other ingredients.
3. Pour into the quiche case. Scatter with the cheese and dot with the butter from the Topping.
4. Place the filled quiche on the heated tray and bake for 25 minutes until puffed and golden brown.
5. Cool for 5 minutes before serving.

SMOKED FISH QUICHE (*Basic* recipe, p 151)
Serves 4

Additional Ingredients
Smoked mackerel fillet *or* 3 oz (75 g) smoked salmon titbits.
Put the flaked flesh at the bottom of the case, then pour in the filling.

Fruit Pies

We give one basic recipe and several variations of that most delectable of desserts – the two-crust fruit pie. (For pictures showing the lining and filling of a two-crust pie see end papers.) You *can* buy ready-to-roll shortcrust pastry, which is quite acceptable but, of course, cannot compare with the home-made recipe we give below.

When making a two-crust pie, it is essential to use a very short and crisp pastry that can be rolled out so thinly that it cooks in the same length of time as the fruit. To make pastry of this kind, it is necessary to use a generous amount of fat (slightly more than half the weight of the flour) and to sweeten the dough with icing sugar (the pastry is much easier to roll out than when caster sugar is used). Various combinations of butter, white fat and margarine will all make successful pie pastry. It is best to experiment and find out which suits you best.

Leftovers
Will keep for 2 days in the larder, 4 days in the refrigerator.

Basic Fruit Pie Pastry
Enough for a two-crust 8 or 9 in (20 or 22·5 cm) pie

Utensils
Sieve; mixing bowl; knife; fork; cup or small bowl; teaspoon; tablespoon; pastry board; film or foil

Ingredients

8 oz (225 g) plain flour
2 level tbsps icing sugar
Pinch of salt
5 oz (150 g) butter or 4 oz
(125 g) butter or hard
margarine and 1 oz (25 g)
white fat

1 egg yolk (keep white for
glazing pie)
1 tsp vinegar
3 tbsps ice-cold water

Method

1. Sift the flour, icing sugar and salt into the mixing bowl and add the fat cut into 1 in (2·5 cm) cubes.
2. Rub in gently with the fingers and thumbs of both hands, until no pieces of fat larger than a small pea come to the surface when the bowl is gently shaken.
3. Using a fork, beat the egg yolk, vinegar and water in the small bowl to blend, then sprinkle over the flour mixture, turning it with a fork or your fingers until all the dry ingredients are evenly dampened.
4. Gather together into a dough which will be firm but pliable.
5. Sprinkle a little flour on the pastry board or the table top, then gently knead the dough with your finger tips for 30 seconds, or until it looks smooth and has no cracks in it.
6. Divide it in two and press each piece into a flattened ball about 1 in (2·5 cm) thick.
7. Wrap in film or foil and chill for at least 30 minutes. This makes the pastry very crisp rather than greasy when it is cooked, and also easier to roll out as the fat will have firmed up.

Basic Apple Pie
Serves 5-6

Use *Basic Fruit Pie Pastry*, p 152

Utensils

Potato peeler; cook's knife; mixing bowl; tablespoon; teaspoon; rolling pin; pastry board; 10 in (25 cm) pie plate or 8 in (20 cm) pie dish 1 in (2·5 cm) deep; pastry brush; fork

Filling

4 large baking apples
4 oz (125 g) granulated sugar
2 tsps cornflour
1 tsp cinnamon
2 tbsps raisins (optional)

Glaze
Egg white (left over from pastry)
2 tsps granulated sugar, to finish

Method

1. Make *Basic Fruit Pie Pastry* and chill.
2. Set the oven at Gas 7, 425°F, 215°C.
3. Peel, quarter and core the apples and cut them into slices $\frac{1}{8}$ in (3 mm) thick.
4. Put them into a bowl and mix with the sugar, cornflour, cinnamon and raisins (if used).
5. Put one of the chilled pieces of pastry on the pastry board (lightly sprinkled with flour).
6. Lightly flour the rolling pin and, using short, sharp strokes, start rolling the pastry into a circle about 11 in (27·5 cm) across.
7. Keep making quarter turns of the pastry, so that the circle is kept even and it does not stick to the board. Do not turn the pastry over as raw flour would then be rolled into both sides and the pastry would be toughened.
8. Carefully ease the pastry circle on to the back of the rolling pin, then lay it gently into position in the pie dish.
9. Spoon in the apple filling.
10. Lift up the dish in one hand, and, holding a sharp knife vertically with the other, cut off the overhanging pastry all the way round. Knead these remains into the second ball of pastry and roll that out in exactly the same way to fit the top of the pie.
11. With a pastry brush or the fingers, dampen the edge of the bottom crust all the way round, then gently transfer the top crust via the rolling pin to fit on top.
12. Press the two crusts together, then using the knife held vertically again, cut off any excess top pastry.
13. Using a dull-bladed knife, nick the two crusts together all the way round, making 'cuts' every $\frac{1}{4}$ in (6 mm). Alternatively, you can 'scallop' the two edges together with the fingers and thumb.
14. Using a fork beat the egg white left over from the pastry until it is frothy, then paint the egg white evenly on top.

15. Scatter with a thin layer of granulated sugar, then make 6 parallel cuts through the centre of the top pastry to allow steam to escape.
16. Bake in the hot oven for 10 minutes, then reduce heat to Gas 5, 375°F, 190°C, and bake for a further 40 minutes, or until the pastry is a rich golden brown.
17. Serve warm or cold.

NOTE: The pie can be reheated; put it in a moderate oven (Gas 4, 350°F, 170°C) for 20 minutes.

SPRING RHUBARB PIE
Serves 5-6

Use *Basic Fruit Pie Pastry* (see p 152)

Filling

1½ lbs forced (pink) rhubarb (washed)
1 oz (1 rounded tbsp) flour
Nut of butter, cut small
½ lb granulated sugar
½ tsp ground ginger

Glaze
Egg white (left over from pastry)
2 tsps granulated sugar

Method
1. Make *Basic Fruit Pie Pastry* and chill.
2. Set the oven at Gas 7, 425°F, 215°C.
3. Trim leaves and 'wings' off rhubarb, wipe and cut into 1 in (2·5 cm) lengths.
4. Put in the mixing bowl with all the filling ingredients and mix well (hands are easiest).
5. Follow instructions for *Basic Apple Pie*, stages (5) to (8).
6. Spoon rhubarb filling into the bottom crust, cover with the top crust as in *Basic Apple Pie*, stages (10) to (13). Glaze with egg white and sugar as described, stages (14) and (15).
7. Bake for 15 minutes, then turn heat down to Gas 4, 350°F, 180°C for 30 minutes, or until the crust is golden, and the filling feels tender when a knife is inserted gently through the top.
8. Serve warm or cold.

GOOSEBERRY PIE
Serves 5-6

Use *Basic Fruit Pie Pastry* (see p 152)

Filling

1½ lbs (700 g) young green gooseberries
7 oz (200 g) granulated sugar
2 level tsps cornflour
2 tbsps water

Glaze
1 egg white (left over from pastry)
2 tsps granulated sugar

Method

1. Make *Basic Fruit Pie Pastry* and chill.
2. Set the oven at Gas 6, 400°F, 200°C.
3. Wash the gooseberries, then top and tail them with a pair of scissors.
4. Mix the sugar and cornflour in a bowl, then add the gooseberries. Toss together gently to coat the gooseberries.
5. Follow instructions for *Basic Apple Pie*, stages (5) to (8).
6. Spoon gooseberry filling into the bottom crust, cover with the top crust as in *Basic Apple Pie*, stages (10) to (13). Glaze with egg white and sugar, stages (14) to (15).
7. Put the pie in the oven, and immediately turn heat down to Gas 5, 375°F, 190°C. Cook for 35 minutes or until golden brown and crisp.
8. Serve only slightly warm or at room temperature. Particularly good with custard or cream.

17. Cakes and Biscuits

Please don't avoid this chapter because you think home-made cakes and biscuits are not worth the effort, and anyhow you haven't the time or spare energy to bake. Even if you've never baked a single cake or biscuit before, you'll be able to put together the very simple recipes we give below. The only technique you need to know is how to stir or beat with a wooden spoon. Yet the results will positively amaze you, and even more your friends, when you offer them these beautiful richly-flavoured tender cakes and crunchy biscuits. (All the recipes in this section have been made under the most primitive conditions – when the mixing has been done in one building and the baking in another!)

NOTE. The 'all at once' cakes can be mixed using a small electric mixer; they will take only 2 minutes instead of 3 minutes.

Basic All-at-Once Cake
6-8 portions

Utensils
8 in (20 cm) deep cake tin or 2 x 7 in (17·5 cm) sandwich tins; pastry brush; greaseproof paper; pencil; mixing bowl; teaspoon; tablespoon; grater (optional); wooden spoon; rubber spatula; cooling tray

Ingredients
4 oz (125 g) soft margarine
4 oz (125 g) caster sugar
5 oz (150 g) self-raising flour and
1 bare tsp baking powder

2 eggs (size 3 or 4)
1 tsp vanilla essence *or* grated rind of ½ lemon or orange
1 tbsp hot water

Method

1. Set the oven at Gas 4, 350°F, 170°C and brush the tins with a very thin layer of oil. If they are not non-stick, it's a good idea to line the bottom with a piece of greaseproof paper. To do this, stand the tin on the greaseproof paper, draw round it with a pencil and then cut out the paper to fit the bottom.
2. Put all the ingredients into the mixing bowl and stir; beat with the wooden spoon for about 3 minutes, or until the mixture is smooth and creamy and a light cream in colour.
3. Use the rubber spatula to transfer it from the mixing bowl to the chosen tin, and smooth the top level.
4. Bake in the preheated oven for 35-45 minutes in the 8 in (20 cm) tin, or for 25-35 minutes in the two 7 in (17·5 cm) tins.
5. When the *minimum* baking time is over, open the oven and quickly press the centre of the cake(s) with your forefinger. If the cake is done it will spring back; if it's not quite done, your finger will leave a slight impression on top so give it the extra time.
6. Remove from the oven and place on the cooling tray. If no cooling tray is available, put it on the grill part of the oven-grill – the idea is to let air circulate all round so the bottom doesn't go soggy.
7. After 5 minutes when it's cool enough to handle, turn upside down and let it gently drop out of the tin(s).
8. You can serve the 8 in (20 cm) cake 'as is' with a sprinkling of caster sugar put on the top whilst still warm, or you can split and sandwich it – as you would the two 7 in (17·5 cm) cakes – with some nice jam.

Leftovers

Store in an airtight tin or plastic container. Goes stale after a week.

FAIRY CAKES (*Basic* recipe, p 157)
15 or 16 individual cakes

Delicious little cakes that save bringing out a big cake when only one or two people drop in for a coffee.

Additional Ingredients
2 rounded tbsp currants or raisins
(You will also need 16 little paper cake cases)

Method
1. Set oven at Gas 6, 400°F, 200°C. Add the currants or raisins to the *Basic All-at-Once Cake* mixture.
2. Put the cake cases 1 or 2 in (2·5-5 cm) apart on a baking tray.
3. Fill the cases with the mixture, ⅔ of the way up.
4. Bake for 15-20 minutes until springy to the touch (see stage (5) of *Basic All-at-Once Cake* recipe).
5. Cool as in *Basic All-at-Once Cake* recipe.

Leftovers
Store in an airtight tin or plastic container. They go stale after 4 days.

CHERRY FAIRY CAKES (*Basic* recipe, p 157)

Make as for *Fairy Cakes* but substitute 2 oz (50 g) sliced glacé cherries for the currants or raisins.

All at Once Chocolate Cake

A moist, tender cake with a superb flavour. You can serve it plain or covered with chocolate icing.

Utensils
8 in (20 cm) deep cake tin or 2 x 7 in (17·5 cm) sandwich tins; pastry brush; greaseproof paper; pencil; mixing bowl; teaspoon; tablespoon; wooden spoon; rubber spatula; cooling tray

Ingredients
4 oz (125 g) soft margarine
4 oz (125 g) caster sugar
4 oz (125 g) self-raising flour
1 level tbsp cocoa
2 level tbsps drinking chocolate

1 tsp baking powder
1 tbsp hot water
1 tsp vanilla essence
2 eggs (size 3 or 4)

Method
1. Set the oven at Gas 4, 350°F, 180°C, lightly oil the tin(s), and line if necessary (see stage (1), *Basic All-at-Once Cake*).

2. Put all the ingredients into the bowl and beat until smooth and creamy – about 3 minutes.
3. Use the spatula to transfer the mixture from the mixing bowl to the chosen tin(s), and smooth the top level.
4. Bake in the preheated oven for 35-45 minutes in the 8 in (20 cm) tin or 25-35 minutes in the two 7 in (17·5 cm) tins.
5. Test as described in stages (5) and (6) *Basic All-at-Once Cake* (see page 158).
6. After 5 minutes when it's cool enough to handle, turn upside down and let the cake(s) gently drop out of the tin.
7. When quite cold, sandwich together and/or top with Milk Chocolate Frosting (see below). If preferred, the 8 in (20 cm) cake can be simply sprinkled with icing or caster sugar and served plain.

All-at-Once Chocolate Frosting

Utensils
Sieve for icing sugar; medium sized bowl; wooden spoon; rubber spatula; teaspoon; small cup

Ingredients
3 oz (75 g) soft butter or margarine
4 oz (125 g) icing sugar

2 tbsp drinking chocolate
1 tsp instant coffee, dissolved in
2 tsp boiling water

Method
1. Put all ingredients into the bowl and beat with the wooden spoon until smooth and fluffy – about 3 minutes.
2. Spread between the layers and on top of the two 7 in (17·5 cm) sandwich cakes and on the top and sides of the 8 in (20 cm) cake. Use a knife to spread, then rough up the top with a fork.

Luscious Lemon Cake

This is a little more complicated than the other cakes, but is so delicious that it's worth the extra effort. You must, however, have a 9 x 5 x 3 in (22·5 x 12·5 x 7·5 cm) loaf tin, *or* you can make Lemon Fairy Cakes, but they're not quite as exciting as the big cake.

Utensils
Loaf tin (see above) or 20 paper cases; greaseproof paper; mixing bowl; wooden spoon; grater; lemon squeezer

Ingredients
4 oz (125 g) soft margarine
6 oz (125 g) caster sugar
6 oz (175 g) self-raising flour
3 tbsps milk
Grated rind of 1 lemon
2 eggs (size 3 or 4)

Lemon Syrup
4 oz (125 g) icing or granulated sugar
4 tbsps lemon juice (1 very large lemon)

Method
1. Set oven at Gas 4, 350°F, 180°C for loaf cake or at Gas 5, 375°F, 190°C for little cakes.
2. Grease the loaf tin (if used), then line the bottom and two narrow ends with a strip of greaseproof paper. Put the paper cases 2 in (5 cm) apart on a baking tray.
3. Put all the cake ingredients into a bowl and beat until smooth and creamy – about 3 minutes.
4. Turn into a loaf tin (if used) and smooth level; or divide between the paper cases, filling each one about ⅔ full.
5. Bake the large cake for 45 minutes, and the little cakes for 15 minutes until they are golden brown and spongy to the touch.
6. While the cakes are cooking, make the lemon syrup; put the ingredients in a small pan and warm together until the sugar has dissolved in the liquid.
7. Put the cooked cake(s) on a cooling tray or grill-rack and prick all over with the fork, then pour the syrup all over the top(s).
8. The little cakes are now ready. The large cake should be left until cold, then carefully tipped out of the tin.
9. Store in an airtight tin or plastic container. Will keep fresh for up to a week.

Basic Streusel Kuchen
12 pieces

This is a spongy Continental-style coffee-time cake which can be topped with a streusel (crumble), or served plain or with fruit. It can be served either as a cake or a pudding. It makes one big cake or two smaller ones, but it's not really worth making a smaller quantity as it will keep well, either in an airtight tin or (in the case of the fruit kuchens) covered in the refrigerator.

Utensils
2 x 7 in (17·5 cm) sandwich tins or 1 x 10 in (25 cm) flan dish; medium sized bowl; wooden spoon; rubber spatula; teaspoon; tablespoon; small bowl; knife

Ingredients
8 oz (225 g) self-raising flour
1 tsp baking powder
3 oz (75 g) soft margarine
3 oz (75 g) caster sugar
1 egg
1 rounded tbsp apricot jam or ginger marmalade (optional but good)

5 fl oz (150 ml) milk
Streusel topping
2 oz (50 g) flour
2 tsp ground cinnamon
2 oz (50 g) butter or margarine
6 oz (175 g) soft brown sugar

Method
1. Set the oven at Gas 6, 400°F, 200°C. Put all the ingredients into the medium bowl and beat until smooth and creamy – about 3 minutes.
2. Use the rubber spatula to turn into the oiled or greased tin(s), smoothing the top level.
3. In the small bowl, mix the streusel topping flour, cinnamon and sugar. Then cut the fat in little bits, and rub into the flour mixture, using the thumb and fingers of both hands. The crumble is ready when it looks like coarse sand.
4. Sprinkle all over the cake(s).
5. Bake for 25-30 minutes or until golden brown and firm to the touch.

NOTE: When stale, this cake is lovely sliced and toasted, then buttered.

Variation

APPLE STREUSEL KUCHEN (*Basic* recipe, p 161)
12 pieces

Additional Ingredients
1½ lb (700 g) baking apples (weight before peeling)

Method
1. Set oven at Gas 5, 375°F, 190°C.
2. Peel, core then quarter the apples, then cut into slices $\frac{1}{8}$ in (3 mm) thick.
3. Make the *Basic Streusel Kuchen*, but before covering with the streusel, arrange the apples in overlapping slices neatly on top of the kuchen mixture, then cover with the streusel.
4. Bake for 40-50 minutes or until the cake has shrunk away from the side of the tin(s), the apples feel tender when pierced with a sharp knife, and the streusel is golden brown.

NOTE: This is at its most delicious 1-2 hours after baking. But it is still very edible for up to 3 days. Store tightly foil-covered in the refrigerator.

To re-heat, foil-cover the whole kuchen or individual pieces and put in a moderate oven (Gas 4, 350°F, 180°C) until warm to the touch, about 15 minutes.

Basic Orange Fork Biscuits
20 biscuits

These biscuits get their curious name because they are shaped by pressing into a disc with the tines of a fork, rather than using the tedious method of rolling them out. They are quite delectable. Butter gives a better flavour and texture than margarine.

Utensils
Medium-sized bowl; grater; knife; baking tray; large fork; cup; metal spatula or knife

Ingredients
5 oz (150 g) self-raising flour
4 oz (125 g) butter cut in 1 in (2·5 cm) chunks
2 oz (50 g) caster sugar
Finely-grated rind of 1 orange
Caster sugar for finishing

Method
1. Set the oven at Gas 4, 350°F, 180°C.
2. Put the flour, sugar and rind in the bowl, add the butter and rub it into the dry ingredients between the fingers and thumb of both hands.
3. When the mixture begins to look a little damp, and begins to cling together, gather it together with your hand into a ball.

4. Pinch off pieces the size of a small walnut and roll between the palms of the hands into little balls.
5. Arrange 2 in (5 cm) apart on the ungreased tray.
6. Fill the cup with cold water, take the fork and dip it in, then press it down on the balls first one way and then another. Biscuits about ⅜ in (1 cm) thick will be formed.
7. Bake for 15 minutes until a pale gold in colour.
8. Remove from the oven and immediately sprinkle with a fine layer of caster sugar.
9. Lift off the tray using the metal spatula of knife and put on a cooling tray or grill rack.
10. Store in a tin or airtight container. They will keep fresh for up to 2 weeks.

Variations

HAZELNUT FORK BISCUITS (*Basic* recipe, p 163)
25-30 biscuits

Use the coarsely-ground hazelnuts that you can get at most health food shops.

Additional Ingredients
2 oz (50 g) coarsely-ground
hazelnuts
½ tsp vanilla essence
Omit grated orange rind and
1 oz butter from *Basic Orange
Fork Biscuits* recipe

Method
1. Set oven at Gas 4, 350°F, 180°C.
2. Make exactly as for *Basic Orange Fork Biscuits*, adding the hazelnuts and essence to the flour mixture.
3. Bake for 10-12 minutes or until golden brown.
4. When cold, store in a tin or airtight plastic container.

Flapjacks
50 pieces

These biscuits are also very easy to make as the mixture is simply spooned into a tin, then cut into fingers when cool.

Utensils
Pan; wooden spoon; $\frac{1}{2}$ in (1·25 cm) deep baking tin, 11 × 15 in
(27·5 × 37·5 cm) or 2 small Swiss roll tins

Ingredients
4 oz (125 g) butter $\frac{1}{2}$ lb (250 g) golden syrup
4 oz (125 g) soft brown sugar $\frac{1}{2}$ lb (250 g) porage oats

Method
1. Set oven at Gas 3, 325°F, 170°C.
2. Melt the butter in the pan over moderate heat, then add the sugar
   and syrup; keep on heating and stirring until the mixture is
   smooth and no sugar grains can be seen.
3. Stir in the oats and mix thoroughly together.
4. Grease the tin(s) lightly, then spoon in the mixture, flattening it
   into a layer about $\frac{3}{8}$ in (1 cm) thick, using wetted hands.
5. Bake for 30 minutes until a rich brown.
6. Cool for 5 minutes and then cut into fingers measuring
   approximately 3 x 1 in (7·5 x 2·5 cm). Remove from the tin
   when cold.
7. Store in an airtight tin. Will keep fresh for up to 3 weeks.

Sesame Seed Crunch

These are made on the same principle as the Flapjacks but are
rather more exciting in flavour and texture because of the variety
of the ingredients – they taste rather like the crunchy cereal one
can buy.

Utensils
Cook's knife; chopping board; pan; tablespoon; wooden spoon;
Swiss roll tin measuring 7 × 11 in (17·5 × 27·5 cm); spatula

Ingredients
2 oz (50 g) hazelnuts   2 oz (50 g) sesame seeds
5 oz (150 g) butter *or* margarine   2 oz (50 g) desiccated coconut
3 oz (75 g) fine brown sugar   6 oz (175 g) porage or rolled
3 oz (75 g) thin honey *or* golden   oats
syrup

Method

1. Set oven at Gas 3, 325°F, 160°C.
2. Roughly chop up the hazelnuts using the cook's knife.
3. Melt butter over low heat, then add the sugar and honey (or golden syrup), the sesame seeds, coconut and the hazelnuts and stir well until they are thoroughly mixed.
4. Spoon the mixture into the tin, then press it level with a spatula.
5. Bake for 25-30 minutes or until a rich golden brown.
6. Cool 10-15 minutes or until the mixture can be cut into fingers about 3 in (7·5 cm) long and 1 in (2·5 cm) wide, using a sharp knife. When quite cold, remove from the tin.
7. Store in an airtight tin or plastic container. Will keep fresh for up to 3 weeks.

NOTE: If mixture becomes too firm before you can cut it, put the tray back in the oven for 2-3 minutes.

18. Fruit Salads and Hot Puddings

By the time it comes to the 'afters', most people are quite satisfied to settle for fresh fruit in one guise or another. It's only in colder weather, or when the main course is a bit 'thin', or you're just plain feeling hungry that something bubbly and hot from the oven takes one's fancy. So in this chapter we suggest a variety of ways of making fresh fruit perhaps a little more interesting, and then some basic hot puddings which you can vary to suit your own taste. The more elaborate desserts are to be found in the *Parties* chapter (see page 194).

Fruit Salads

A bowl of assorted fresh fruits or, more dramatic, just one bowl of a choice fruit in season – be it satsumas, or grapes, apples or strawberries – is the perfect finish to almost every meal.
However, it is important that whatever fruit you serve should be in choice condition. The safest way to achieve this is to serve only what's in season – because then it will be both flavourful and relatively cheap. The more expensive seasonal (but perishable) fruits such as grapes, peaches or melons can often be bought at knock-down prices on Saturday afternoon, as the greengrocer won't want to keep them over the weekend. Strawberries and other berries are often cheapest on half-closing day presumably because there's *only* half a day's trading in which to sell them. Only berries need to be eaten within 24 hours (eat them the same day if you can't refrigerate them); other perishable fruit will keep for another 24 hours in a cool larder, or up to 3 days in the refrigerator. We always keep apples in the refrigerator because they don't need any further ripening and they taste better when slightly chilled. But all fruits that do need to ripen – melons, pears, peaches – are best kept at room temperatures until they're ripe, and then refrigerated until required.

It's very difficult to put into words the technique of judging ripeness as different varieties of the same fruit demand different treatment. Generally, however, the following holds true: *bananas* are ripe when they develop brown patches on the yellow skin; *pears* when they give very gently all over; *melons* give slightly when pressed at the stem end and develop a musky flavour; and *peaches* have areas of blush pink and feel very slightly soft all over.

For the rest, find yourself a reliable greengrocer and ask his advice.

Pineapple or Melon Boats

If you're looking for the simplest method of serving, then just cut wedges or slices, remove the seeds or core and tuck in. But for a slightly more elegant presentation, try this.

Utensils
Knife with serrated edge; chopping board

Method
1. Cut the fruit down the centre in two halves, then divide each half into curved slices, each about 1½ in (3·5 cm) thick at the skin end.
2. Take each 'boat shape' in turn and cut out the woody core (in the case of the pineapple) and remove the seeds (in the case of the melon). Now cut as close as possible to the skin so that the slice of fruit is freed from it. Leave this slice on the skin and cut it down at 1 in (2·5 cm) intervals.
3. Then push alternate chunks of the fruit about ½ in (1·25 cm) out of line.
4. The pineapple needs no further treatment, but the melon can be sprinkled with a squeeze of lemon juice and then a teaspoon of sugar (caster if you have it) and chilled for an hour.
5. You can then eat the fruit with a knife and fork, or pass tooth picks and spear each section of fruit in turn. So simple, but so delicious.

Basic Lemon Syrup for Fruit Salad
Enough for 4-6 helpings

The perfect fruit salad should have a happy balance between the sweetness of the fruit and the sugar or syrup with which it is usually mixed and the tartness of lemon or lime juice that should be added. All fruit salads, however, improve immeasurably if left for a few hours before eating – this allows an exchange of flavour to take place between the fruit and the liquid in which it is steeping. If you don't want to make a syrup as I suggest, simply cut up your fruit then sprinkle it with the juice of a lemon and perhaps 2 tbsps of sugar (caster preferred). Stir gently to blend, cover and leave at room temperature for an hour so that the sugar will draw the natural juices out of the fruit. After that, put in a cool place until required.

But the following syrup, as a basis for any fruit salad, is particularly good for juicy fruits such as oranges and soft fruit.

Utensils
Small pan; tablespoon; lemon squeezer (or strong hand)

Ingredients

3 oz (75 g) granulated sugar	Any juice that comes out of fruit
Juice of 1 large lemon	(particularly oranges) as you
	prepare them

Method
1. Put the sugar and the lemon juice into the pan and heat until the sugar is dissolved and the mixture goes clear.
2. Cut up the chosen fruit, adding any juices to the syrup.
3. Put the fruit in a serving bowl and pour the syrup over.
4. Leave for an hour, when you will find that the natural juices of the fruit will have been drawn out and there will be just enough of a not-too-sweet or tart syrup with the cut up fruit sitting in it.
5. Chill if possible.

Leftovers
Fruit salad should be eaten within 24 hours as the fruit goes soggy and may go 'fizzy' as it starts to ferment.

SPRING FRUIT SALAD
Serves 4-6
Additional Ingredients

4 oranges	¼ lb (125 g) black grapes
3 bananas	

Method
1. Prepare *Basic Lemon Syrup* (pp 168-9).
2. Peel the oranges with a serrated knife, rather as if they were apples, cutting round and round through both the skin and the pith until the flesh is revealed (keep your fingers well out of the way of the knife).
3. Now cut with the knife in between the sections so that the orange falls out into a bowl and the pith is left behind.
4. Squeeze this 'skeleton' with your hand and let the juice go into the syrup.
5. Peel and slice the bananas ½ in (1·25 cm) thick. Halve and pip the grapes.
6. Put all the fruit in a serving bowl and pour the syrup over.
7. Leave for an hour at room temperature, then chill (if possible) for several hours.

SUMMER FRUIT SALAD
Serves 4

For the time in late June or early July when strawberries are at their best. Or get them from a PYO (pick your own) farm – not necessarily any cheaper but definitely in their prime.

Additional Ingredients

2 tbsps cold water
1 lb (450 g) strawberries
2 large bananas, sliced

1 orange, sectioned (see previous recipe)

Method
1. Halve the strawberries if large and put in a heatproof bowl or casserole.
2. Make the *Basic Lemon Syrup* (pp 168-9) but add the water to it and bring to the boil.
3. Immediately pour over the strawberries – this will set the colour as well as bring out their juice.
4. Add the sectioned orange and sliced bananas and leave for an hour. Then put in a cool place until required.

AUTUMN FRUIT SALAD
Serves 4-5
Additional Ingredients

2 tbsps cold water
1 tbsp raspberry jam
1 large orange
1 large peach

1 large Comice pear
4 dessert plums
1 small very ripe melon

Method
1. Make *Basic Lemon Syrup* (pp 168-9), adding extra water and raspberry jam. Bring to the boil.
2. Section the orange (as for *Spring Fruit Salad*). Slice the peach and pear (skin or not as you prefer). Cut up the plums and discard the stones, halve the melon, cut in sections, cut away skin, remove pips then make ¾ in (2 cm) cubes.
3. Put in bowl, with any juices. Pour hot syrup over the fruit.
4. Leave for 1 hour, then chill until required.

WINTER FRUIT SALAD Serves 4-5

Additional Ingredients

Small can pineapple titbits
1 tbsp apricot jam
2 large oranges

1 apple
1 ripe pear
1 banana

Method
1. Drain the juice or syrup from the pineapple and add to the ingredients for the *Basic Lemon Syrup* (pp 168-9) together with the jam. Put the pineapple into a heatproof dish or casserole.
2. Peel and cut up the oranges (as for *Spring Fruit Salad*). Halve then quarter the apple, remove the core section, then cut in ⅛ in (3 mm) thick slices. Put in the heatproof dish.
3. Peel and slice the pear and the banana. Put in the heatproof dish.
4. Bring the *Basic Lemon Syrup*, the juice and the jam to the boil, then pour over the fruit.
5. Leave at room temperature for 1 hour, then chill until required.

APPLE COMPÔTE
Serves 4-5

If you like, you can stew the apples in the syrup until they 'fall'

---

and become almost a purée. But if you like separate slices of apple swimming in the syrup, either use the cheapest eating apples available or use baking apples cut in thick slices and watch them carefully so that you take them off the heat before they fall. Either way, this is a lovely mixture, gorgeous with custard or ice cream.

Utensils
Frying pan with lid; serrated-edge knife; tablespoon; wooden spoon

Additional Ingredients

1-1¼ lbs (450-575 g) Bramley baking or any dessert apples
4 tbsps water
2 tbsps orange juice

1 small tbsp apricot jam
2 tsps grated lemon rind
¼ tsp ground cinnamon or
1 cinnamon stick

Method
1. Peel the apples, cut in quarters then cut out the core section.
2. Cut the baking apples into slices 1 in (2·5 cm) thick, the eating apples ½ in (1·25 cm) thick.
3. In the pan put the ingredients for the *Basic Lemon Syrup* (pp 168-9), together with the water, orange juice, jam, rind and cinnamon.
4. Heat gently, stirring with the wooden spoon until the sugar and jam have dissolved, then boil for 3 minutes until the syrup looks as thick as that in canned fruit.
5. Carefully put in the apple slices – if possible in one layer, otherwise lay them gently in two layers.
6. Bring to the boil, then reduce the heat until the liquid is barely bubbling, cover and cook very gently for 10 minutes or until the fruit is soft when pierced with a knife.
7. Baste well with the syrup half-way through (tip the pan so that the syrup runs to one side and you can spoon it over the fruit).
8. When the fruit is tender, baste it once again with the syrup, then put on the lid and leave until it's cold – about 1 hour.
9. Chill until required.

Leftovers
Unlike some other fruits, apples will keep for at least 2 days in a cool larder, 4 days in the refrigerator.

SPICED PEARS IN BROWN SUGAR
Serves 4

This is a lovely way to cook the hard (and usually reasonable in price) Conference pears that are available mainly in the autumn and winter.

Utensils
Frying pan with lid; potato peeler; serrated-edge knife; wooden spoon

Additional Ingredients
¼ tsp powdered *or* 1 stick cinnamon

4 tbsps water
4-6 pears

Method
1. Peel the pears (easiest with a potato peeler), then halve and remove the little bit of core and pips.
2. Put the *Basic Lemon Syrup* (pp 168-9), made with brown sugar instead of white, together with the water and cinnamon, into the pan and bring to the boil, stirring to help the sugar dissolve in the liquid.
3. Now lay the pear halves in it, side by side. Baste with the syrup as in *Apple Compôte* and bring to the boil, then reduce the heat until the syrup is barely bubbling.
4. Cover and simmer for 15 minutes, or until the pears feel tender when pierced with a small knife.
5. Baste once more during the cooking time.
6. Take off the heat and leave in a cool place for several hours.

Leftovers
Will keep 4 days in the refrigerator, 2 days in a cool larder.

Hot Fruit and Puddings

In this section, we give the basic method of baking apples because it's easy, reasonable in price and extremely good to eat. As for hot *puddings*, we have limited these to two kinds – crumbles and sponges. These again are easy to make with the minimum of equipment and give pleasure far out of proportion to the labour involved.

Basic Baked Apples

Utensils

Apple corer; serrated-edge knife; teaspoon; tablespoon; baking dish about 2 in (5 cm) deep, large enough to hold apples side by side

Ingredients, per person

1 baking apple
1 tbsp raisins

1 tsp brown or white sugar
water
1 tbsp golden syrup

Method

1. Set oven at Gas 4, 350°F, 180°C.
2. Core the apple(s), then cut through the skin round the 'equator' of the apple(s) – this stops it exploding if it gets too hot.
3. Arrange in the baking dish. Fill the hole where the core was with raisins and top with the sugar.
4. Pour round the apples enough water to come to a depth of just under ½ in (1·25 cm).
5. Dribble the golden syrup over each apple in turn.
6. Scatter the remaining raisins in the liquid in the dish.
7. Bake in a moderate oven for 1 hour, basting once or twice with the juices in the dish.
8. Take the apples out of the oven when you start to eat the main course – they are better served warm rather than hot.
9. Serve plain, or with ice cream or custard.

Leftovers

Will keep 2 days in the larder, 4 days (covered) in the refrigerator.

Variation

APPLES BAKED IN ORANGE SYRUP

Additional Ingredients, per person

Small nut of butter
1 tbsp brown sugar

Orange juice

Omit water and golden syrup from *Basic Baked Apple* recipe

Method
1. Set oven at Gas 4, 350°F, 180°C, and prepare apples as described in *Basic Baked Apples* stage (2) and (3).
2. Top each apple with the nut of butter and 2 tsps of the brown sugar.
3. Instead of water, pour orange juice (fresh or from a carton) on to the bottom of the baking dish and scatter with the remainder of the brown sugar and raisins.
4. Bake in the moderate oven for 1 hour, basting once. Serve warm.

Basic Apple Crumble
Serves 4-6 once, 2-3 twice
This is one of those brilliantly simple ideas that gives a marvellous result far out of proportion to the effort involved. Sliced fruit is topped with a crumble mixture made in a similar way to pastry but without any water to bind it, and no need to roll it out.

Utensils
1½ pint (850 ml) ovenproof dish; apple peeler; knife; tablespoon; mixing bowl

Ingredients

3 large baking apples
1 tbsp lemon juice
5 tbsps water
2 oz (50 g) sugar
½ level tsp cinnamon

Crumble topping
3 oz plain brown or white flour
1 oz porage oats
3 oz soft brown sugar
3 oz margarine or butter

Method
1. Set oven at Gas 5, 375°F, 190°C.
2. Peel, quarter, core and slice the baking apples into the ovenproof dish.
3. Mix the lemon juice with water and sprinkle over the fruit, finally topping with the sugar and cinnamon mixed.
4. For the topping, put the flour and the oats into a bowl, cut the fat into 1 in (2·5 cm) chunks, then gently rub into the dry ingredients by rubbing them between the fingers and thumbs of both hands, separately.
5. When the mixture has become an even, crumbly mass, sprinkle it in an even layer over the fruit in the dish.

6. Bake in the oven for 40-50 minutes or until crunchy and golden brown.
7. Serve plain, with custard, or with ice cream.

Leftovers
Will keep 2 days in larder, 4 days (covered) in the refrigerator.

DAMSON CRUNCH (*Basic* recipe, p 175)
Serves 4 once, 2 twice

Additional Ingredients
5 fl oz (150 ml) water   or medium can (approximately
3 oz (75 g) sugar   15 oz (425 g) damsons
1 lb (450 g) damsons
Omit apple filling from *Basic Apple Crumble* recipe; make topping in the same way

Method
1. Set oven to Gas 5, 375°F, 190°C.
2. Put water and sugar into a saucepan, and heat until sugar dissolves, then boil for 3 minutes.
3. Add the damsons, bring back to the boil, then cover and simmer until tender – about 5 minutes. When cool, remove the stones gently.
4. Arrange the stewed fruit in the bottom of a heatproof dish, and spoon on enough juice to cover to a depth of $\frac{1}{4}$ in (6 mm).
5. Top with the crumble topping from *Basic Apple Crumble* recipe, and bake in the same way.

Note
Leftover *Apple Compôte* (see page 172) can be mixed with the damsons to give them a little body.

RHUBARB AND GINGER CRUMBLE (*Basic* recipe, p 175)
Serves 4 once, 2 twice

Additional Ingredients
1 lb (450 g) rhubarb   1 oz (25 g) chopped hazelnuts
3 oz sugar   (optional)
1 tsp ground ginger
Omit apple filling from *Basic Apple Crumble* recipe; make topping with hazelnuts (if used)

Method
1. Set oven at Gas 6, 400°F, 200°C.
2. Trim leaves and 'wings' from rhubarb, and wipe. Cut into 1 in (2·5 cm) lengths, and arrange in an ovenproof dish.
3. Sprinkle with the sugar mixed with the ginger.
4. Make the crumble topping as for the *Basic Apple Crumble*, stirring in chopped hazelnuts if used.
5. Bake for 30 minutes, or until crunchy and golden brown.

Bread and Butter Pudding Serves 4-5

This is a simple, but delicious rib-sticker on a cold day. Start the pudding about 2 hours before you want to eat it.

Utensils
Bread knife; buttering knife; tablespoon; wooden spoon; 1½ pint (850 ml) casserole

Ingredients

Butter or margarine	2-3 tbsps currants or other
Brown sugar	dried fruit
6 thin slices white bread or	1 pint milk
bun loaf buttered	2 tbsps custard powder
	2 tbsps caster sugar

Method
1. Set oven to Gas 3, 325°F, 170°C.
2. Use a bit of greaseproof or kitchen paper as a pad to grease the inside of the dish with a little butter or margarine, then sprinkle it with brown sugar. This gives a lovely crusty finish to the underneath and sides of the pudding.
3. Cut the bread into strips about 1 in (2·5 cm) wide and arrange in layers, sprinkling a little brown sugar and dried fruit between each layer.
4. Make the custard with the milk, powder and caster sugar according to the directions on the tin (it should be of a thin, pouring consistency) and pour it slowly down the side of the bread.
5. Leave to stand for half an hour. This allows the bread to soak up the custard and gives it the characteristic delicious spongy texture when it is baked.

6. Sprinkle with a little more brown sugar, then bake in the oven for 1½ hours, increasing the heat at the end if necessary to brown the top.

Leftovers
Will keep 1 day in the larder; 3 days (covered) in the refrigerator.

Basic Baked Apple Sponge
Serves 4-5 once, 2-3 twice

This is a light sponge pudding made by the 'all-at-once' or 'one-stage' method (no creaming or rubbing-in), with any variety of stewed or canned fruit underneath.

Utensils
Mixing bowl; wooden spoon; apple peeler; tablespoon; teaspoon; knife; spatula; 1½ pint ovenproof casserole

Ingredients

1 lb (450 g) baking apples	*For the sponge*
1 tbsp lemon juice	3 oz (75 g) soft margarine
3 tbsps water	3 oz (75 g) caster sugar
2 oz (50 g) sugar	5 oz (150 g) self-raising flour
	½ tsp baking powder
	1 egg
	1 tbsp hot water

Method
1. Set oven at Gas 4, 350°F, 180°C and smear the inside of the casserole with a thin layer of butter or margarine.
2. Peel the apples, quarter and cut out core sections, then slice as thinly as possible into the greased casserole.
3. Pour over the lemon juice and water and sprinkle with the sugar.
4. Put all the sponge ingredients into a bowl and beat together for 2 minutes until the mixture is smooth and creamy in appearance.
5. Spoon over the fruit and smooth level with the knife or spatula.
6. Bake in moderate oven for 45-50 minutes until golden brown in colour and firm to gentle touch with a finger.
7. Serve plain, or with custard or ice cream.

PLUM OR DAMSON PUDDING (*Basic* recipe, p 178)
Serves 4-5 once, 2-3 twice
Additional Ingredients
5 fl oz (150 ml) water
3 oz (75 g) sugar

1 lb (450 g) damsons or plums
or medium can (approximately
15 oz or 425 g) damsons or plums

Omit apple filling from *Basic Baked Apple Sponge* recipe; make
topping in the same way.

Method
1. Set oven at Gas 6, 400°F, 200°C, and grease inside of
   casserole.
2. Put water and sugar into pan, and heat until sugar dissolves,
   then boil for 3 minutes.
3. Add the damsons or plums, bring back to the boil, then cover
   and simmer until tender – about 5 minutes. When cool,
   remove the stones gently.
4. Put fruit and juice into casserole as for *Basic Baked Apple
   Sponge*, and make sponge topping.
5. Spread the sponge topping on top and bake in oven for 30
   minutes.
6. Sprinkle the top with sugar before serving. Nicest with hot
   custard.

Milk Puddings

Once considered only 'nursery' food, milk puddings are now back
in favour. You can buy a wide selection ready-to-eat in cans, but
if you have access to an oven it is much cheaper (and tastier) to
make your own. The secret of success is to cook the pudding very
slowly in a low oven.

Rice Pudding
Serves 4

Utensils
Sieve; ovenproof dish; tablespoon

Ingredients
2 level tbsps pudding
(short-grain) rice
Butter for greasing pudding dish

1 pint (575 ml) milk
1 level tbsp granulated sugar
Pinch ground nutmeg (optional)

Method
1. Put the rice in the sieve and put under the cold tap until the water runs clear. Drain well until no water is coming out of the rice.
2. Butter the ovenproof dish well, using a butter paper or your finger. Add the milk and then the rice, and stir.
3. Leave for half an hour for the rice to soften in the milk.
4. Add the sugar and stir well. Sprinkle with nutmeg (if used).
5. Bake in a slow oven (Gas 2, 300°F, 150°C) for at least 2 hours, though longer is even better. The pudding should have a golden brown skin on top, and be soft and creamy inside.
6. Serve plain or with stewed fruit.

Sago or Semolina Pudding
Serves 4

Utensils
6 in (15 cm) saucepan; tablespoon; wooden spoon; 1 pint (575 ml) pudding dish

Ingredients
1 pint (575 ml) milk   1 level tbsp granulated sugar
2 level tbsps sago or semolina

Method
1. Rinse out the pan with cold water (this stops milk sticking).
2. Add the milk and warm until it starts to steam.
3. Sprinkle the sago or semolina on top, stirring constantly.
4. Keep on stirring until the milk comes to the boil, then add the sugar.
5. Lower the heat, and cook very gently for 20 minutes, stirring occasionally to stop it catching on the bottom.
6. Serve plain or with jam or stewed fruit.

19. Party Food

Everyone has their own idea of what constitutes a party – and that applies equally to the two authors of this cookbook, as one would expect considering the generation gap. So we're not laying down any rules for parties, just giving you a selection of recipes that we've found useful for everything from coffee for half a dozen to a stand-up drinks party for fifty. On the way there are recipes for simple dinner parties and supper for half a dozen close friends.

When it comes to organizing a party there is only one piece of advice we think is worth passing on – give the kind of party at which you yourself feel at home.

Preparations
It's easy to calculate how much food you need for eight people; it can get a bit out of hand when you're up to fifty! So here's a good rule of thumb: when catering for over twenty-five deduct one in every five servings. So that, instead of making fifty servings for fifty people of any particular recipe, you would make forty servings. For a hundred people you would make eighty servings. This is particularly helpful at a buffet where there are a number of dishes offered.

Wine quantities
At a drinks party, allow a third to a half bottle per person, but this isn't a hard and fast rule – *you* know your friends' capacities. So if possible have reserve stock on a 'sale or return' basis.

Useful food quantities
Allow ¾-1 oz of crisps per person for a drinks party.

1 long French bread, 18 in (45 cm) long, cuts into 50-60 slices for canapés.
1 x 7 oz (200 g) packet of savoury crackers contains 40-50.
1 large sliced loaf contains approximately 25-30 slices, according to the thickness.
½-¾ lb sliced meat or poultry and 1 large sliced loaf make approximately 50 small sandwiches (¼ of a large slice).

Making sandwiches in advance
Always cover tightly with film or foil and refrigerate or leave in a cool place.

Open French bread canapés — make up to 4 hours in advance.
Closed sandwiches — make up to 4 hours in advance.
Savoury cracker or toast canapés — make up to 1 hour in advance.

Meatless Main Courses
Lentil Roast
Serves 6

This is served at King's College, Cambridge, and is made to the recipe of a former student. It is quite delicious and can be used as a vegetarian main course dish.

Utensils
Large bowl for soaking lentils; sieve; small roasting tin or casserole dish approximately 10 x 8 x 2 in (25 x 20 x 5 cm); cook's knife; chopping board; garlic press; measuring jug; teaspoon; grater

Ingredients
11 oz (300 g) red lentils
1 lb (450 g) onions
4 oz (125 g) butter
1 fat clove of garlic crushed *or*
¼ tsp garlic powder
1 tsp mixed herbs or Italian seasoning herbs

10 fl oz (275 ml) cold water
2 tsps Marmite
9 oz (250 g) grated Cheddar cheese
4 tbsps bought browned crumbs

Method
1. The night before put the lentils into a bowl and cover with twice their depth of cold water.

2. Next day (or when ready to make the roast), turn into a sieve and run water through until it is clear. Leave in sieve to drain. Grease the tin or casserole, and light oven at Gas 2, 300°F, 150°C.
3. Peel, halve then chop the onions coarsely.
4. Melt the butter in the frying pan and cook the onion and garlic (if used) until golden brown.
5. Add the water and Marmite, then remove from the heat.
6. Add half the cheese, the herbs and garlic powder (if used), as well as the drained lentils. Taste and add up to 1 tsp salt if necessary.
7. Mix well then turn into the buttered tin or casserole dish.
8. Mix the remaining cheese with the breadcrumbs and sprinkle on top. Bake in oven for 2 hours until crusty. Serve in squares.

Spanish Omelette
Serves 4-6

A good dish for when you arrive home at the same time as your guests. An entire main course is in the frying pan and only needs bread and butter to accompany it.

Utensils
Frying pan; cook's knife; tablespoon; teaspoon; fork; grater

Ingredients

6 eggs (size 2 or 3)	1 large red pepper, halved,
½ tsp salt	de-seeded and cut in thin strips
10 grinds black pepper	4 large canned (or fresh)
1 tbsp water	tomatoes
Filling:	½ tsp salt
2 oz (50 g) butter or 3 tbsps oil	10 grinds black pepper
1 medium onion finely chopped	1 tbsp chopped parsley
Sprinkle of garlic salt	1 tsp dried Herbes de Provence
4 oz mushrooms thinly sliced	3 oz grated sharp cheese

Method
1. Whisk the first 4 ingredients together with the fork until the yolks and whites are evenly blended.
2. Prepare the vegetables.
3. Melt the butter or oil in the frying pan and the minute it stops foaming add the onions, garlic salt, mushrooms and red pepper slices.

4. Cook gently until the onion is a rich golden brown, then add all the remaining ingredients (except the egg mixture and grated cheese).
5. Cook until the tomatoes have softened and the mixture is thick but still juicy.
6. Pour on the egg mixture and cook, tilting the pan until no free egg remains on top, about 3 minutes.
7. Sprinkle the omelette thickly with the grated cheese and put under a very hot grill until golden brown and well puffed.
8. Serve at once from the pan.

Swiss Eggs
Serves 4-5

An easy but delicious lunch or supper dish.

Utensils
1 shallow ovenproof dish, large enough to hold the eggs side by side; cook's knife; grater

Ingredients
2 oz (50 g) butter
Several slices of Gouda or Edam cheese
8 eggs

5 fl oz (150 ml) single cream
Nutmeg, salt and pepper
2 oz (50 g) finely grated cheese (any kind)

Method
1. Set the oven at Gas 5, 375°F, 190°C. Spread the butter thickly over the bottom of a shallow ovenproof dish, then cover completely with the thin slices of cheese.
2. On to this carefully break the eggs.
3. Pour the cream over the eggs and sprinkle with salt, pepper and nutmeg, then with the grated cheese.
4. Bake for 10 minutes, then place it briefly under a very hot grill until the cheese is brown.

Vegetable Risotto
Serves 8

Utensils
Cook's knife; chopping board; frying pan or saucepan with lid; tablespoon; teaspoon; oven casserole (optional)

Ingredients

2 medium onions
2 large red peppers
1 lb (450 g) mushrooms
2 tbsps oil
2 oz (50 g) butter
2 tsps salt
10 grinds black pepper
Pinch garlic salt
1 lb (450 g) Italian risotto rice

28 oz (800 g) tin Italian tomatoes
Pinch paprika
Pinch dried basil
1½ pints (850 ml) boiling water
or vegetable stock
4 tbsps raisins or sultanas
1 can flaked tuna *and/or* 4 oz
(125 g) grated cheese, to finish

Method

1. Prepare vegetables: peel and chop onions; halve peppers, de-seed, then cut in ½ in (1·25 cm) squares; slice mushrooms.
2. In saucepan or frying pan heat oil and butter till butter melts.
3. Add chopped onion, cover and fry for 5-10 minutes till soft and golden.
4. Add peppers and mushrooms, salt and pepper and garlic salt. Fry for further 5 minutes.
5. Add rice, toss in fat and vegetables, and fry for 5 minutes till rice becomes opaque.
6. Add remaining ingredients except sultanas.
7. Bring to boil, then cover and simmer over very gentle heat for 30 minutes. (If more convenient, can be transferred to casserole and cooked in oven at Gas 4, 350°F, 180°C for 30 minutes or until all liquid has been absorbed.)
8. Add raisins or sultanas, fluff with fork.
9. Serve topped with flaked tuna and/or grated cheese and accompany with salads and wholemeal bread.

Aubergines Stuffed with Tuna
Serves 6
A very savoury, quickly prepared summer meatless main dish.

Utensils
Cook's knife; tablespoon; teaspoon; can opener; frying pan with lid; ovenproof casserole large enough to hold the aubergine halves, side by side; small basin

Ingredients

3 8 oz (225 g) glossy aubergines
2 tbsps oil
1 large onion, finely chopped
1 clove garlic, crushed
15 oz can tomatoes, drained
1 tsp mixed dry Italian seasoning
or 1 tbsp chopped fresh herbs
(including basil and parsley)

1 tbsp tomato purée
½ tsp salt
10 grinds black pepper
1 tsp brown sugar
1 7½ oz (200 g) tin tuna fish
2 tbsps dry breadcrumbs
1 oz (25 g) melted butter or
margarine
4 oz (125 g) grated cheese

Method

1. Set oven at Gas 5, 375°F, 190°C. Cut the aubergines in half lengthways.
2. Using a spoon, carefully remove the inside flesh, leaving a ½ in (1·25 cm) thick layer of raw aubergine in the shell.
3. Chop the removed aubergine flesh roughly, and prepare the other vegetables.
4. Heat the oil in the frying pan, then add the onion and cook covered until soft and golden.
5. Add the garlic, tomatoes, herbs, purée and aubergine pulp, together with the salt, pepper and sugar.
6. Cover, bring to the boil and simmer for 20 minutes.
7. Drain and flake the tuna, then add to the cooked mixture.
8. Arrange the aubergine halves side by side in a casserole, then divide the mixture between them.
9. Mix the crumbs and melted fat, then add the cheese. Divide this mixture between the aubergines, arranging it roughly over the filling.
10. Cover and cook for 35 minutes or until the aubergine feels tender when pierced with a sharp knife. If the top is not a rich brown, put under the grill for 3 minutes. (If your casserole has a glass lid, it will brown through it.)

Tuna Lasagne
Serves 6-8

A magnificent supper dish that is actually better if made the day before, then reheated. Don't be put off by the ingredients; it's simple to make, and there is no need to pre-cook the pasta.

Utensils
Small saucepan; cook's knife; chopping board; lidded saucepan; teaspoon; tablespoon; batter whisk; lasagne dish or roasting tin 12 x 8 x 2 in (30 x 20 x 5 cm); grater; can opener

Ingredients
12 strips of green or plain lasagne

Sauce

3 eggs	1 level tsp mustard
1 medium onion	¼ tsp ground nutmeg
1 medium green pepper	1½ level tsp salt
2 7 oz (200 g) cans tuna	¼ tsp white pepper
3 oz (75 g) butter or margarine	4 oz (125 g) grated cheese
3 oz (75 g) plain flour	4 tbsps single cream *or*
1½ pints (850 ml) milk	top of milk
	1 tbsp chopped parsley

Method
1. Put eggs in small saucepan to hard-boil (see p 40).
2. Set oven at Gas 5, 375°F, 190°C.
3. Peel, then finely chop the onion. Halve the peppers, de-seed, and cut into tiny dice.
4. Drain tuna and flake; slice the hard-boiled eggs.
5. Melt the butter in the larger saucepan; cook the onion in it, covered, for 5 minutes until softened. Add the pepper, cover and cook for a further 3 or 4 minutes.
6. Uncover the pan, stir in the flour, followed by the milk, mustard, nutmeg, salt and pepper.
7. Whisk until bubbly, simmer 3 minutes, then stir in 3 oz (75 g) of the cheese, the cream or top of milk, parsley, tuna and hard-boiled egg slices.
8. Butter the lasagne dish, and put a thin layer of the sauce on the bottom. Cover with 4 strips of lasagne, then sauce.
9. Repeat twice, ending with a thin layer of sauce.
10. Cover with the remaining cheese.
11. Bake for 40 minutes, until a rich bubbly brown. If possible, leave overnight then reheat at same temperature for 25 minutes or until bubbly. Cut in squares to serve.

Leftovers
Keep one day in the larder, 3-4 days covered in the refrigerator.

Meaty Main Courses

To Roast a Joint of Meat

Your family may have its traditional method of roasting (there are probably at least 30 methods being used throughout the country) but research commissioned by the Meat Promotion Executive and carried out by the Meat Research Institute has shown that the most consistently good results are achieved by the following method.

Utensils
Roasting tin; rack (optional); slotted spoon; tablespoon; teaspoon; large bowl or foil

Method
1. Have the joint weighed, either by the butcher or at home, as it will be for cooking (i.e. on the bone, or boned *less* bones and trimmings).
2. Preheat the oven, so that it is at the right temperature when the meat is put in.
3. Use oven setting of Gas 3, 325°F, 170°C for *all meat*, and cook for times as given below.

	Rare	Medium	Well-done
Beef	20 mins per lb (45 mins per kg) +20 mins	25 mins per lb (55 mins per kg) +25 mins	30 mins per lb (67 mins per kg) +30 mins
Lamb	—	25 mins per lb (55 mins per kg) +25 mins	30 mins per lb (67 mins per kg) +30 mins
Pork	—	—	30 mins per lb (67 mins per kg) +30 mins

(Most people like to cook pork well, and few like lamb rare.)

4. Allow joint to rest for 15-20 minutes after completion of cooking time. This can be done in the switched-off oven with the door ajar, or by dishing the meat and covering with foil or a large bowl. The

resting period makes the meat much easier to carve, and it will be more evenly cooked.

Basting

With the slow method of roasting described here, there is no need to baste the meat. However, if yours is a very lean joint, paint it all over with oil (1 tbsp per pound or 450 g of meat) before putting it into the oven. Before painting on the oil, added flavour and a crunchy crust can be achieved by sprinkling the meat with black pepper and dry mustard. (Add salt after cooking, otherwise the salt will draw out too much juice.)

Gravy

To produce a rich brown gravy without using gravy browning, slice an onion, then arrange it around the meat before it goes into the oven – this will caramelize during the cooking period, and give a wonderful colour and flavour to the drippings at the bottom of the roasting tin from which the gravy is made. Remove the onion before making the gravy (it's delicious to eat with other vegetables).

Drain off three-quarters of the fat at the bottom of the tin, then add to the tin a stock cube and twice as much water as you want of finished gravy (allow about 2 tbsps gravy per serving). Bring to the boil on top of stove over direct heat, stirring the mixture well to loosen the delicious meat extracts adhering to the tin. Bubble until reduced by half. Season well. This gravy can be made just before a meal, then transferred to a small pan to keep hot.

NOTES:

1. A foil covering will slow down the rate of cooking. Meat which is to be well done should not be wrapped in foil, as this prevents the meat reaching the recommended final internal temperature. Strictly speaking, covering the cooking container, covering in foil, or cooking in a roasting bag is *pot roasting*; the times given above will not be relevant.
2. The lower oven temperature given here reduces spitting and keeps the oven cleaner.
3. The shape of the cut will affect the cooked result: e.g. a long thin cut will take less time to cook than a round boned and rolled cut.
4. The roasting dish should be about 1½-2 in (3·5-5 cm) deep

and just large enough to hold the joint, but not so large that there is a lot of uncovered surface which may cause the fat to overheat. Joints on the bone (rib roast, lamb shoulder or leg) are placed directly in the tin. Rolled and boned joints (sirloin, rib) are best put on a meat rack to prevent them frying in the fat at the bottom of the dish. However, the rack is not absolutely vital.

To Grill Lamb Chops

Lamb chops are expensive in relation to mince or stewing meat, but they are very quick and easy to cook and there may be times when you feel the cost is justified. This is how to get the best possible result.

Utensils
Shallow dish wide enough to hold the required number of chops side by side; teaspoon; tablespoon; fork

Ingredients

2 grilling chops
2 tsps oil
Pinch garlic salt
5 grinds black pepper
¼ tsp salt

¼ tsp each dried basil and rosemary (or ½ tsp Italian seasoning herbs)
1 tsp lemon juice

Method
1. An hour before the chops are to be grilled, put the oil into the shallow dish and stir in the garlic salt, black pepper, salt, herbs and lemon juice.
2. Put the chops into the dish and turn to coat them with the flavoured oil.
3. Leave them in the oil for an hour, turning them once or twice so that they are really steeped in the flavourings.
4. 15 minutes before you intend to eat, put on the grill and heat it for 5 minutes.
5. Arrange the chops on the grid of the grill pan so that heat can circulate all the way round and they're not sitting in the oil which drips off them.
6. Put the grill pan 4 in (10 cm) below the source of heat and grill for 5 minutes on each side until a rich brown just cooked through.

7. Eat at once.

NOTE: The herbs can be omitted, but they do improve the flavour.

Meat Loaf
Serves 6-8

This is equally delicious served hot or cold.

Utensils
Small basin; baking tin large enough to hold meat loaf (see stage 4); mixing bowl; grater; fork; tablespoon; teaspoon

Ingredients

3 large slices of bread
1 medium onion
2 eggs
1 level tbsp porage oats
2 lb (900 g) finely minced raw meat
1 tsp dry English mustard

1 generous tbsp tomato ketchup
1 tbsp soy sauce
1 tsp Herbes de Provence *or* Italian seasoning
2 level tsps salt
15 grinds black pepper

Method
1. Set oven at Gas 7, 425°F, 215°C. Put the bread in a basin, cover with cold water and leave 5 minutes to soften; then drain off water and squeeze the bread as dry as possible.
2. Grate the onion, beat the eggs, then add to the bread and mix with a fork until smooth.
3. Turn this mixture into the mixing bowl and add the oats, the meat and all remaining ingredients, then stir with a large fork till thoroughly and evenly blended.
4. Arrange in a loaf shape about 2 in (5 cm) high and 3 in (7·5 cm) wide in the centre of the baking tin, which should be just enough to hold it with a 2 in (5 cm) margin all round.
5. Put in the oven for 15 minutes to brown, then turn down to Gas 4, 350°F, 180°C for a further 35 minutes until richly brown. Serve hot or cold.

Leftovers
Keep 2 days in the larder, 3 days (covered) in the refrigerator.

Lamb and Potato Braise
Serves 4-6

This can be cooked in a frying pan on top of the stove, so it makes it ideal if your cooking facilities are limited.

Utensils
Potato peeler; cook's knife; bowl; chopping board; paper or plate for flour; tablespoon; teaspoon; fork; frying pan with lid

Ingredients
1½ lb (700 g) potatoes
1 large onion
4-6 large lamb chops (any kind)
2 tbsps flour
1 level tsp salt
10 grinds black pepper
½ tsp paprika

3 tbsps oil
½ tsp dried oregano
2 tsps tomato purée *or* ketchup
½ bayleaf
8 fl oz (225 ml) thin gravy *or* chicken stock

Method
1. Peel the potatoes, cut in slices about ⅜ in (1 cm) thick and leave covered with cold water. Peel the onion, then cut in half and then into paper thin slices.
2. Trim the fat off the chops and dip in the flour mixed with the salt, pepper and paprika. Brown really well in the oil in the frying pan. Remove and drain on tissue or kitchen paper.
3. In the same oil, cook the onion until it is soft and golden (about 5 minutes), then sprinkle with the herbs and the ½ bayleaf and pour in the gravy or stock (made from a cube) with the purée or ketchup.
4. Stir well together, then add the drained potatoes in one layer, laying the browned chops on top of them.
5. Cover tightly either with a lid or foil and simmer very gently for one hour on top of the stove.

NOTE: The ingredients can be arranged in the same way in an oven casserole and cooked for 1½ hours at Gas 2, 300°F, 150°C. By the time the chops are tender the potatoes will be soft and have absorbed much of the delicious gravy.

Pineapple Beef
Serves 6

A good dish for a cold winter's day.

Utensils
Cook's knife; chopping board; frying pan; slotted spoon; fork; tablespoon; teaspoon; oven casserole

Ingredients
3 tbsps oil

2 lb (900 g) braising or stewing steak, cut into 1 in (2·5 cm) cubes

1 medium onion

3 sticks celery

1 medium can (14 oz or 400 g) pineapple chunks

½ pint (275 ml) beef stock, made with a bouillon cube

2 level tsps salt

10 grinds black pepper

2 level tbsps cornflour

1 tbsp soy sauce

1 tbsp tomato ketchup

2 tbsps vinegar

Method
1. Set oven at Gas 2, 300°F, 150°C, and prepare vegetables. Peel and coarsely chop the onion, wash and slice the celery.
2. Put the oil in the frying pan, and when you can feel the heat on your hand held 2 in (5 cm) above the surface of the pan, add the meat and cook until brown on all sides.
3. Add the chopped onion and sliced celery and continue to cook for a further 5 minutes, until the vegetables have wilted and absorbed most of the fat.
4. Drain the juice from the pineapple and make it up to 10 fl oz (275 ml) with water. Add with the stock, salt and pepper to the meat.
5. Transfer to the oven casserole and cook for 2 hours or until the meat is almost tender.
6. Mix the cornflour with the soy sauce, ketchup and vinegar and stir into the meat with the pineapple chunks.
7. Cover and cook a further 20 minutes.

NOTE: If preferred, the mixture can be simmered in a pan top of stove for 2 hours.

Leftovers
Keep 1 day in larder; 3-4 days covered in a refrigerator.

Southland Barbecued Chicken

Serves 6-8

Everybody's favourite chicken casserole. A tangy tomato sauce
turns chicken into a party dish. The sauce is sufficient to cook 1
large bird cut into 8 joints, or two smaller (3¼ lb or 1·5 kg) birds
each cut into four.

Utensils

Cook's knife; chopping board; frying pan; oven casserole;
tablespoon; teaspoon; fork; can opener

Ingredients

6-8 chicken joints
2 oz (50 g) butter or margarine
2 tbsps oil
1 onion
2 level tsps salt
¼ tsp freshly ground black
pepper

2 level tbsps fine brown sugar
2 tsps prepared mustard
1 tsp Worcestershire sauce
Juice of ½ lemon
5 oz (150 g) can tomato purée,
diluted with 2 cans water

Method

1. Set oven at Gas 4, 350°F, 180°C.
2. Peel and chop onion finely.
3. Dry the chicken joints well, then fry in the butter (or margarine)
   and oil until golden all over. Remove to the casserole.
4. Fry the onion in the remaining fat until soft and golden (about
   5 minutes), then add all the remaining ingredients.
5. Simmer for 5 minutes, then pour over the chicken.
6. Cover and bake in oven for 1 hour.
7. This dish is better if refrigerated or left in a cool place
   overnight, then heated through until bubbly in a moderate
   oven.

Desserts

Marbled Strawberry Cream

Serves 6

A beautifully simple, delicious dessert. You must give the
strawberries time to make their juice, as well as allowing time for
the dessert to set.

Utensils

Shallow bowl or dish; tablespoon; liquid measure; lemon squeezer; bowl; glass serving dish

Ingredients

1 lb strawberries   Juice of ½ lemon
2 tbsps caster sugar   10 fl oz (275 ml) natural yogurt
1 packet strawberry jelly

Method

1. Slice the strawberries and put them in a shallow bowl. Sprinkle with the caster sugar, and leave in a cool place for at least an hour (they will make delicious juice).
2. Make up jelly to 1 pint (575 ml) according to packet directions, then stir in the lemon juice.
3. Put into larger bowl to chill until syrupy, then stir in the sugared strawberries and the yoghurt (it should have a marbled effect).
4. Put it into the bowl you will serve from (glass is best, as it shows off the marbling) and leave to chill until set.

Orange Venetienne

Very simple, very refreshing, after a meat or chicken casserole

Utensils

Serrated-edge knife; grapefruit knife; teaspoon; tablespoon

Ingredients per person

1 very large orange   Lemon juice
Caster sugar   any orange-flavoured liqueur

Method

1. Cut a tiny slice off the base of each orange so it will balance on the serving plate.
2. Cut a 'cap' off the orange about a third of the way down.
3. Prepare the fruit itself as if it were a grapefruit, loosening the sections with a grapefruit knife and removing the centre core of pith.

4. Fill this core with caster sugar and pour on enough lemon juice to saturate the sugar.
5. Sprinkle the fruit itself with liqueur (omit if you haven't any).
6. Replace the top of each orange and chill for not more than an hour. Eat with a teaspoon.

Spiced Bananas
Serves 6-8

Utensils
Frying pan; serrated-edge knife; liquid measure; teaspoon; tablespoon

Ingredients
6-8 large bananas (one per person)
scant 3 oz (75 g) butter
5 fl oz (150 ml) orange juice

3 tbsps lemon juice
½ tsp ground cinnamon
1 oz chopped hazelnuts *or* almonds, preferably toasted

Method
1. At least 30 minutes before you want to eat, split the skin of each banana lengthwise and place on a baking sheet.
2. Bake in moderately hot oven (Gas 6, 400°F, 200°C) for 15 minutes or until the skin turns black. Leave in the skins.
3. In a heavy frying pan melt the butter over gentle heat, then add all the remaining ingredients.
4. Bubble fiercely, stirring, until a thick but juicy sauce is formed – about 3-4 minutes.
5. Peel the bananas and put them in the sauce, basting well and turning until coated.
6. *To serve:* Lift the bananas on to a serving dish and spoon the sauce over them. Decorate with toasted chopped hazelnuts or almonds. Serve at room temperature, plain or with slightly whipped cream.

NOTE: The hot baked bananas are delicious served plain with a sprinkling of sugar and lemon juice.

Pears in Spiced Cider
Serves 6-8

A dish that looks as good as it tastes.

Utensils
Covered saucepan; cook's knife; tablespoon; teaspoon; potato peeler

Ingredients

6-8 medium-sized pears (such as Conference)
1 pint (575 ml) medium dry cider
3 oz (75 g) caster sugar
1 level tbsp dark brown sugar (if possible)

$\frac{1}{2}$ tsp ground cinnamon
Juice of a small lemon
$\frac{1}{4}$ pint whipping cream (optional)

Method
1. Peel the pears, but leave them whole – including the stem.
2. Put the cider into the pan, and add the sugar and spice with half the lemon juice, bring to the boil.
3. Add the whole peeled pears, baste well, cover and simmer until tender but not mushy (15-30 minutes), basting twice with the syrup. Test by piercing with a sharp knife.
4. Lift out and arrange the pears, stalks up, in a dish.
5. Bring the liquid to the boil again and simmer for 5 minutes until the flavour has intensified and the syrup has greatly reduced in volume.
6. Add the remaining lemon juice, and pour over the pears.
7. When cold, leave in a cool place or in the refrigerator.
8. Serve with the cream flavoured with 2 tsps extra caster sugar and a pinch of ground cinnamon, then whipped until it holds soft peaks (a batter whisk is excellent for this job).

Butterscotch Sauce for Ice Cream
Makes 12 portions

This will keep for as long as you let it in the refrigerator. Serve hot (when it's liquid) or cold (when it's thick).

Utensils
Small pan; wooden spoon; tablespoon; teaspoon

Ingredients

6 oz (175 g) brown sugar
4 tbsps golden syrup
2 oz (50 g) butter

6 oz (175 g) can unsweetened evaporated milk
1 tsp vanilla essence

Method
1. Place all the ingredients in a small saucepan and heat gently until blended into a smooth cream. *Do not boil.*
2. Serve warm or cold over ice cream.

Chocolate Sauce for Ice Cream

This will keep indefinitely in the refrigerator or for a week in the larder. Serve warm over ice cream. The sauce can be made in advance, then reheated.

Utensils
Sieve; small saucepan; tablespoon; wooden spoon

Ingredients

3 oz (75 g) butter or margarine   1 small can (6 fl oz or 175 ml)
8 oz (225 g) sieved icing sugar   unsweetened evaporated milk
3 oz (75 g) cocoa

Method
1. Over gentle heat, melt the fat in the saucepan.
2. Add the sugar and cocoa and 2 tbsps of the milk, stirring well.
3. Add the remaining milk gradually, constantly stirring to keep the mixture smooth, and bring to the boil.
4. Continue to stir and simmer gently for 3 minutes.
5. Serve from a jug or bowl.

Party Pieces

Syrian Cheese Puffs
Serves 12, allowing 2 per person

It's helpful to have two people making these delectable little morsels if you're making huge quantities as there's a lot of rolling and cutting pastry. But it's worth it. The puffs can be frozen uncooked in advance (for 3 months) or refrigerated for up to 48 hours beforehand. Try and serve them freshly baked. Do not reheat as they will go tough. They keep warm for up to 30 minutes after baking. (To make enough for 50 people, see *Note* below.)

Utensils
Grater; mixing bowl; fork; small bowl; rolling pin; pastry board or plastic table top; 3 in (7·5 cm) pastry cutter; teaspoon; tablespoon; baking trays; pastry brush

Ingredients
½ lb (225 g) Cheddar cheese
2 eggs
Pinch salt

Sesame seeds
¾ lb (350 g) ready-made puff pastry (a large packet)

Method
1. Allow pastry to thaw, if necessary.
2. Grate the cheese finely into mixing bowl. Using fork and small bowl whisk the eggs to blend yolks and whites. Reserve 2 tbsps egg for glazing the puffs.
3. Add the remainder of the eggs to the cheese with the salt to make a sticky paste.
4. Following the instructions on the packet, roll out the pastry to the thickness of a knife blade, then cut with cutter into approximately 25 rounds.
5. Place a tsp of the cheese filling in the centre, dampen the edges of the pastry then fold over and seal into a half moon.
6. Arrange on baking trays which have been dampened with cold water.
7. Brush with reserved egg. Leave while you set the oven to Gas 7, 425°F, 220°C.
8. When the oven is at temperature, brush the puffs again with the remaining egg and scatter with the sesame seeds.
9. Bake for 15 minutes until a rich brown.

NOTE: If you want to make *Syrian Cheese Puffs* for 50, use 2½ lbs (1·1 kg) puff pastry, 2 lbs (900 g) Cheddar cheese, 6-7 eggs and 1 level tsp salt. Reserve 4 tbsps egg for glazing, and cut pastry into approximately 100 rounds.

Hot Herb Bread

Utensils
Cook's knife; chopping board; bread knife; small bowl; wooden spoon; tablespoon; teaspoon; ordinary knife; foil

Ingredients

1 level tbsp of a mixture of
chopped fresh herbs (parsley,
chives, basil) *or* 1 level tbsp
fresh parsley
1 long French loaf

3 oz (75 g) soft butter
1 tsp mixed dry herbs
½ tsp paprika
10 grinds black pepper
2 tsps lemon juice

Method

1. Chop fresh herbs finely.
2. Cut the bread into slanting slices just under ½ in (1·25 cm) thick, but do not cut through the base of the loaf (it is left in one piece, rather like a huge comb).
3. Beat the butter to a soft cream, the consistency of mayonnaise, then beat in all the remaining ingredients.
4. Insert this mixture into the loaf, spreading thickly on one side of each slice of bread, then lay the loaf on a piece of foil large enough to enclose it completely.
5. Spread any remaining herb butter mixture on the surface of the loaf.
6. Fold the foil over to seal the loaf completely.
7. Refrigerate until required. About 30 minutes before you want to serve it, put it in a moderately hot oven (Gas 6, 400°F, 200°C) for 20 minutes, then fold back the foil and bake for a further 5 minutes to crispen the crust.
8. Serve hot. Each guest tears off his/her own portion.

NOTE: The bread can be frozen, ready to bake, for up to a week. If the bread is to be baked from frozen, allow an extra 10 minutes baking before folding back the foil.

Dips

These are very useful as party 'ice-breakers' – it's hard not to get acquainted when you're dipping into the same pot.

For 'dippers', use crisps, savoury (but not cheesy) biscuits, and/or *crudités*– an assortment of raw vegetables cleaned, then cut into strips about 2 in (5 cm) long and ⅜ in (1 cm) wide. For 12 people you would need approximately 2 large carrots, 2 green peppers and a heart of celery made into *crudités*, together with a large packet of crisps and a small packet of biscuits.

Put the dips in a bowl set on a large plate, and surround with the *crudités*, crisps and biscuits.

Hummus
Serves 12 as a dip

This Middle Eastern delicacy is made with chick peas, but don't
be despondent – there are excellent cans and packets of mix
which need only a little extra seasoning. If you can get it, pitta
bread torn in pieces is delicious as a 'dipper' for hummus.

Utensils
Can opener; tablespoon; small mixing bowl; rubber spatula

Ingredients
15 oz (425 g) can hummus with   Pinch garlic salt
tahina   ½ tsp salt
3 tbsps lemon juice   10 grinds black pepper
2 tbsps oil (olive or corn)

Method
1. Put the hummus in a bowl, and stir in remaining ingredients.
2. Leave for several hours for flavours to develop.

NOTE: Reconstitute *packeted* hummus. You may find, according
to what make you use, that no further seasoning is necessary.
Otherwise, add some of the ingredients listed above until you like
the taste.
   Take-away hummus, ready to eat, is available in some
delicatessens – but is naturally much dearer.

Cream Cheese Dip
Serves 12 as a dip

You can add almost any savoury ingredient – chopped pepper,
gherkin, olives, celery – to this mixture as the cream cheese
merely acts as a 'carrier' for the other flavourings.

Utensils
Mixing bowl; cook's knife; chopping board; wooden spoon;
teaspoon

Ingredients

½ lb (225 g) medium- or low-fat cream cheese
2 tsps finely chopped fresh herbs (parsley, chives, a little mint) *or* 1 tsp dried mixed herbs
Pinch salt

Pinch nutmeg
10 grinds black pepper
Pinch garlic salt
Small carton natural unsweetened yoghurt

Method

1. Put the cheese in the mixing bowl.
2. Chop the fresh herbs, if used, and stir into the cheese together with all the other seasonings.
3. Add enough yoghurt to make a mixture the consistency of whipped cream.
4. Pile into a bowl and surround with *crudités*, biscuits and crisps.

Leftovers

Keep covered 1 day in a larder cupboard, 3-4 days in a refrigerator.

Italian Honeyed Dip

Serves 12 as a dip

An amazing mixture of flavours, but quite delicious. As it's a bit runny, it's perhaps best served sitting round a table.

Utensils

Mixing bowl; tablespoon; teaspoon; serving bowl (small)

Ingredients

2 rounded tbsps mayonnaise
1 level tbsp thick honey
4 shakes Worcestershire sauce

2 tsps brandy (optional)
Few drops lemon juice

Method

1. Put the mayonnaise in the mixing bowl and add all the remaining ingredients, stirring well.
2. Spoon into the serving bowl and leave for several hours for the flavours to develop.
3. Serve with *crudités* and crisps.

Leftovers
Keep covered 1 week in a larder cupboard, several months in a refrigerator.

Yoghurt Soup
Serves 6

A delightful yet easy recipe for a summer's day.

Utensils
Mixing bowl or large jug; cook's knife; chopping board; tablespoon; teaspoon

Ingredients

½ pint (275 ml) milk
1 pint (575 ml) natural
unsweetened yoghurt
or ¾ pint (425 ml) yoghurt
plus 5 fl oz (150 ml) soured cream
½ cucumber
15 radishes
2 tbsps snipped chives

2 heaped tbsps snipped fresh dill
or 1 heaped tbsp chopped fresh
parsley
Few leaves of fresh tarragon *or*
½ tsp dried tarragon
6 leaves fresh mint *or* ¼ tsp
dried mint

Method
1. Mix the milk, yoghurt and the soured cream, if used (the cream is richer but less refreshing on a hot day).
2. Peel the cucumber and cut into matchsticks, finely slice the radishes, snip the chives and dill (if used) and chop the fresh parsley (if used) and the tarragon.
3. Stir everything into the yoghurt mixture.
4. If too thick (it should be like unbeaten whipping cream), thin with a little more milk.
5. Serve very cold with hunks of brown bread.

Summer Wine Cup
Serves 10-12 with two glasses each

This is potent, so serve in wineglasses not tumblers.

Utensils
Large bowl for mixing; liquid measure; serrated-edge knife or potato peeler; tablespoon

Ingredients

2 litres white wine such as Riesling
1 pint (575 ml) apple juice or sweet cider
1 small can pineapple titbits

1 glass each vodka *and* orange liqueur (optional)
Fresh mint, if available
1 lemon

Method

1. Mix together all the ingredients except the lemon.
2. Take the lemon and, with a sharp knife (or a potato peeler), start at the stalk end to remove the peel, peeling round and round like an apple. Keep the peel in one piece, and leave it anchored to the other end of the fruit.
3. Float the lemon in the punch bowl; the loose peel will spiral prettily round the fruit.
4. Serve well chilled.

Winter Gluhwein

This is a marvellous spiced wine, an 'ice breaker' for a winter party. Borrow the largest pan you can, or a slow-cooker, to heat the drink. It makes enough for 2 4 fl oz (125 ml) glasses each.

Ingredients for 25		Ingredients for 50
4 litres	any cheap red wine	7½ litres
1¾ pints (1 litre)	water	4 pints (2½ litres)
1 tsp	cinnamon	2 tsps
¼ lb (125 g)	sugar	½ lb (250 g)
12	cloves	24
¼ tsp	ground nutmeg	½ tsp
Peel of 1	large orange	Peel of 2
1	sliced lemon	2
¼ pint (150 ml)	Cointreau (optional)	½ pint (275 ml)

Method

1. Dissolve the sugar in the water with the spices, orange peel and sliced lemon.
2. Simmer 5 minutes, then add the wine.
3. Taste and keep on adding extra sugar if necessary until the taste is right.
4. Add the Cointreau and cover; leave at steaming point (just below boiling) for about an hour.
5. Serve from the pan.

Index

Eggs: buying, 39; storing, 24-5, 39-40. *Dishes:* boiled, 40; cheese sauce and, 52; fried, 40-1; salami and, Chinese style, 94; scrambled, 41-4; Swiss, 184 *see also* Omelettes
Electrical appliances, 15

Fairy cakes, 158-9
Fish: buying, 57; storing, 24, 57. *Dishes:* casserole, stove top, 85; fried in batter, 58; grilled, 59-61; Mornay, 55; pie, 55-6; Provençale, 77-8; quiche, 152 *see also* Herring, Mackerel, Trout, Tuna fish
Flans, savoury (quiches), 146-52
Flapjacks, 164-5
Food poisoning, 19-20, 22, 23, 135
Food processors, 15
Frankfurter scrambled eggs, 44
Freezers, 19
French dressing, 122-3
Fritters, cream cheese, 105-6
Fruit: storing, 27. *Dishes:* pies, 152-6; puddings, 173-7, 178-80; salads, 167-73; yoghurt, 108
Frying pans, electric, 15

Gooseberry pie, 156
Goulash, 86
Grapefruit, 27
Grapes, 28
Gravy, 189-90
Greek salad, 128-9

Hazelnut fork biscuits, 164
Herb bread, 199-200
Herbs, storing, 29-30
Herring, spicy grilled, 60
Honeyed dip, Italian, 202
Hummus, 201
Hygiene, 19-20

Ice cream, sauces for, 197-8
Implements *see* Utensils
Italian honeyed dip, 202

Kettles, electric, 15

Lamb: braised with potato, 192; chops, grilled, 190; roasting, 188
Larders, 20, 23-31
Lasagne, tuna, 186-7
Lemons, 27: cake, 160-1; syrup, 168
Lentil roast, 182-3
Liquid measures, 11
Liver risotto, 139-40

Macaroni, 144: casserole, 54; cheese, 53

Mackerel: grilled, 60-1; with scrambled eggs, 44
Marbled strawberry cream, 194-5
Measurements and measuring, 9, 11
Meat: roasting, 188-90; storing, 23; *see also following entries*
Meatballs, 67-70
Meatloaf, 191
Melons, 27, 167: boats, 168
Milk, 25: puddings, 179-80
Mince: buying, 62; storing, 62. *Dishes:* 62-70: basic savoury, 62-3; Spanish rice, 63-4
Mushrooms, 29: quiche, 148; with scrambled eggs, 43

Noodles, 144, 145
Nutrition, 16-19

Olive and cheese quiche, 150-1
Omelettes, 39: cheese, 46, 47; chicken liver, 49; crouton, 46; mushroom, 48-9; onion, 47-8; potato, 47; Spanish, 183-4
Onion vinaigrette, 123
Oranges, 27: biscuits, 163-4; Venetienne, 195-6
Ounce equivalents, 11
Ovens, automatic, 15

Parsleyed noodles, 145
Party food, 181-204: preparations, 181; quantities, 181-2
Pasta, 142-5: types of, 142-3
Pastry: fruit pie, 152-3; quiche, 146-8
Peaches, 167
Pears, 27, 167: spiced in brown sugar, 173; spiced in cider sauce, 196-7
Peppers: ragoût, 84; rice salad and, 132; sautéd, 119-20
Pies, 152-6
Pineapples, 27: boats, 168; with beef, 193
Pizzaiola sauce, 72-3
Plum pudding, 179
Pork, roasting, 188
Potatoes, 29: baked, 114-15; fried, 116; lamb braise and, 192; mashed, 116-17; sautéd with aubergine, 80
Poultry, storing, 23-4
Pressure cookers, 15

Quiches, 146-52; cases for, 146-8

Ragoût, tomato, 71-2
Raisin and carrot slaw, 126
Raita, 109
Refrigeration, 18, 19, 20, 22-31
Rhubarb: crumble with ginger, 176-7; pie, 155

Rice: general information on, 134-5; *Dishes:* boiled, 136; fried, Chinese style, 137-8; fried, Italian style, 136-7; Indian style, 139; Korean, 141; salad, 133; salad with pepper, 132; salad with tuna, 131-2; savoury, 138-9; Spanish, 63-4: tomato soup and, 37-8; *see also following entries*
Rice puddings, 135, 179-80
Risotto, 135, 139-40, 141-2, 184-5
Roasting meat, 188-90

Sago, 180
Salade Niçoise, 129-30
Salads, 121-33; dressings for, 109, 121-3; refrigeration, 18; *see also following entries*
Salad spinner, 121
Salad vegetables, storing, 29-30
Salami and eggs, Chinese style, 94
Salmon quiche, 149-50
Sandwich-makers, 15
Sausages: fried, 111; risotto, 141; scrambled eggs, 44
Semolina pudding, 180
Sesame seed crunch, 165-6
Shopping, 21-2
Slow-cooker, 15
Smoked fish quiche, 152
Soups, 32-8, 203
Spaghetti, 143-4: bolognese, 74-6
Spoons, 9, 11
Spring mince ragoût, 66
Spring stew with dumplings, 88-9
Sprouts, 113
Steak: braised Italian fashion, 73-4; fried, 109; 'poor man's', 70
Stews and casseroles, 82-9
Stir-fried food, 90-7
Store cupboard, 30-1
Storing food, 20, 22-30
Strawberries, 167

Strawberry cream, 194-5
Streusel kuchen, 161-3
Strudel, meat, 66
Summer fruit salad, 170
Summer rice salad, 133
Summer soup, 34-6
Summer wine cup, 203-4
Syrian cheese puffs, 198-9

Tablespoons, 9
Tangerines, 27
Teaspoons, 9
Toast, French, 106
Toasts, cheese, 51-2
Tomatoes, 29: ragoûts, 71-81; salad, Cyprus, 123-4; sautéd with courgette, 118-19; soup with rice, 37-8
Trout with almonds, 59
Tuna fish: aubergines and, 185-6; cheese rice and, 54-5; lasagne, 186-7; macaroni casserole with, 54; quiche, 149-50; salad, 130; salad with rice, 131-2
Turkish meatballs, 69-70

Utensils, 9, 10, 12-15

Vegetables: storing, 18, 28-30. *Dishes:* curry, 82-3; green, basic cooking, 112-14; risotto, 184-5; soup, 36-7; stir-fried, 91-2; stir-fried sweet and sour, 93-4
Vinaigrette, 122-3
Vitamins, 18, 19

Weighing, 9, 11
Wine: cups, 203-4; quantities, 181
Winter fruit salad, 171
Winter Gluhwien, 204
Winter soup, 32-4

Yoghurt dishes, 108-9; soup, 203

To grease a baking tin

Put oil in small bowl. Dip in pastry brush, and shake off excess

Cover all inside surfaces with thin film of oil

If no brush, make small ball of kitchen or tissue paper

Shake off excess, then use circular motion to grease all internal surfaces

To form dough into balls

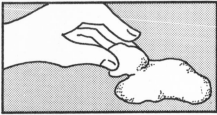

Pick up a piece of dough of whatever size recipe requires

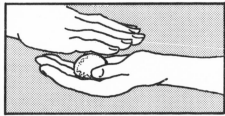

Hold dough in palm of one hand, slightly cupped. Cover with palm of other hand and roll with hands going in opposite directions

To line a flan tin

Roll chilled pastry to circle 3in over diameter of tin, ⅛in thick

Fold over rolling pin to lift; lay gently in tin

Press into shape of tin, using backs of fingers

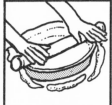

Run rolling pin over sharp-edged tin to trim

Or hold knife vertically in one hand and trim, turning tin

Prick all over bottom surface and sides

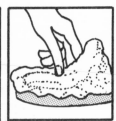

Line with foil. Cover sides and top edge, and press into shape of flan

If possible chill several hours before baking